When the Odds Are Against You

**Stories of real couples
who quit fighting long enough
to begin talking and listening**

Recovery of Hope Series

When the Odds Are Against You

Stories of real couples
who quit fighting long enough
to begin talking and listening

Recovery of Hope Series

Steve Wilke
Dave & Neta Jackson

New Leaf Press

New Leaf Press
First printing: April 1995

ISBN: 0-89221-287-X
Library of Congress Catalog: 94-69842

While the stories in this book are true, the names and other identifiable details of the characters have been changed.

Contents

Introduction

Today our daughter, who recently re-turned to college after a four-week winter break, had one of those "terrible, horrible, very bad, no good" days. First of all, she'd been dreading going back to an unpleasant roommate situation, and was trying to de-cide which was more stressful: to stick it out or go through all the hassle of making a change. Then, when she arrived at school, she discovered that her phone had been cut off because (said the phone company) of an unpaid bill. ("I was sure I'd paid it!" . . . Grrr. Another hassle.)

So after only two days of second semes-ter, she was already feeling a little stressed. When she finally fell asleep last night, she slept hard — right through her alarm this morning, missing a very important class. Upset at herself, she tried to contact the teacher — which was next to impossible because he didn't have an office on campus and she had no phone.

So the bulk of her day was spent trying to track down the missing phone payment . . . trying to locate her teacher and find out what she'd missed in class . . . and talking to her advisor about switching roommates — all before driving 30 minutes to her part-time job.

That's when she discovered that her car — parked "for just a few minutes" in a No Parking zone — had been towed away.

It was the last straw. All the seams holding college life together seemed to be unraveling at once.

The old saying, "When it rains, it pours," aptly describes this phenomena when troubles pile up, one after the other, until a person feels buried under all the mud and sludge.

But our college student's "terrible, no-good day" will probably sort itself out and soon be forgotten. Unfortunately, some people wade through a downpour for months . . . even years. Their marriages — maybe like yours — are besieged with a host of problems and complexities. For Couple A, childhood traumas and abuse carry over into adult relationships, confusing the issues, compounding "normal" struggles, and making it next to impossible to sort out fears from realities. Couple B's family seems "jinxed" with more than their share of heartache and stress: a handicapped child, the death of another, an illness or accident, financial loss or debt — and maybe a catastrophe such as a house fire thrown in for good measure.

When the odds are against you, a person tends to become wrapped up in his or her own pain and despair, unable to reach out in understanding to his or her spouse, who is also desperately hurting. And so husband and wife move in lonely isolation, drifting further apart, adding even more stress to the fabric of life. All the seams of the marriage seem to be unraveling at once.

• • •

When we got the tearful phone call today (from a pay phone), we realized our daughter was experiencing a painful reality: when struggling with numerous problems all at once, it can feel like the whole world is conspiring against you. With so many "big" problems, it's easy to get careless about the little things — e.g., parking in a No Parking zone — and suddenly it's not just raining, it's pouring! But our college student had one thing going for her: she wasn't avoiding the problems. She was trying to keep her priorities straight, doing what she had to do to address each one. When one more problem reared its ugly head (No car! How do I get to work?! I don't have enough money!) she felt stuck, overwhelmed. But with a little help — some TLC, some extra bucks to get her car out of hock — we knew she could beat the odds.

But what about those couples overwhelmed by numerous problems, drowning in the downpour? Maybe someone you love is in that situation. Maybe it describes your own marriage. Is divorce the only solution? Is there any hope?

We believe there is. But don't listen to us. Listen to the two couples who share their true stories in this book — couples whose marriages were drowning in problems so overwhelming and complex, it wasn't just pouring, it was a flood! Spend a little while with these two couples who not only are still married, but are growing in their marriages . . . against all the odds. They are willing to share their stories to give you a glimpse of the same hope that rescued their marriages.

Each couple has participated in Recovery of Hope, a program sponsored by a network of counseling centers around the country. Every day, marital conflicts are resolved, hurts healed, brokenness made whole — but most people do not hear about these successes. And because they do not hear the accounts of restored marriages, they have no hope when their marriage gets in trouble.

The Recovery of Hope Network has helped hundreds of couples recover hope in their marriage primarily by giving them an opportunity to hear other couples, who have been through the worst, tell their stories of reconciliation. The message is clear: With help, marriages *can* be restored.

Throughout the book and especially in the third chapter, Dr. Steve Wilke, a licensed clinical psychologist and former president of Recovery of Hope Network, Inc., provides insights into how various problems feed on each other and create new ones. He also highlights how forgiveness can generate hope, hope can open the doors to openness and honesty, living openly and honestly can give courage to take steps forward in faith — the prerequisites for rebuilding a damaged relationship "when the odds are against you."

Dave and Neta Jackson

Chapter One

To Dream the Impossible Dream

Judy Myers turned slowly to the side, studying her reflection in the big three-way mirror. The wedding dress whispered and rustled as she moved this way and that. The lace bodice with the long, tapered sleeves accented the youthful slenderness of her body. Then the tulle skirt rippled in several tiers to the new, fashionable "theater length:" higher in front than in back, creating a short train. Short, dark hair framed large, brown eyes bright with anticipation and cheeks flushed with excitement.

If only Russell could see her!

"What? I don't even get a peek?" Russell had pouted last night when she'd told him she was going shopping for her wedding dress — without him. He was dressed like other 20 year olds in 1956: hair slicked back into a ducktail, shirt sleeves rolled up to show his bulging arm muscles, skinny belt holding up his trousers.

"Sorry," Judy giggled. "The groom isn't supposed to see the dress till the bride walks down the aisle."

"But that's next August — four months away!" he protested. Then he tilted his head and let his eyes rove admiringly over the soft, yellow angora sweater and long, gray, pleated skirt she was wearing. "I know," he said impishly, "let's skip the wedding and go straight to the honeymoon."

"Russell!" she scolded. She didn't like it when he teased like that. He was supposed to be her knight in shining armor, protecting her from all the Tom, Dick, and Harrys who often hinted that they'd like a fling. "Don't let my parents hear you talk like that."

Now, in front of the mirror, a tiny smile tugged at the corners of her mouth as she imagined how Russell's eyes would light up when she came down the aisle. The mirror silently confirmed what others had always told her: she was beautiful. She looked like a movie star, or a princess!

Like a princess. . . .

She suddenly turned with a worried look to her mother, who was frowning over a wayward thread hanging from the hem.

"Mother, do you think Daddy will like it?" Judy asked anxiously.

"Mmm? Of course . . . why wouldn't he?" Mrs. Myers said absently, bending down to snip the thread.

Of course. Why wouldn't he? Judy echoed to herself as changed back into her street clothes. Her father often complimented her on the way she dressed, her choice of clothes, makeup, and hair style. She'd always been his "little princess." Of course he would like this beautiful dress.

It was just that . . . ever since she got engaged to Russell Warner, her father had seemed a little more withdrawn. Nothing she could really put her finger on. But they'd always had such a special relationship. He'd often confided in her, lavished time and affection on her. Now something felt strained. Still, he seemed to like Russell okay, and he said he was happy for her. But . . . how did he really feel about her getting married?

"Hey, don't worry about it!" Russell had teased a few weeks ago when she wished out loud that her father could be a little more excited about their wedding plans. "You're his only daughter, for Pete's sake. Heck, you're his only kid, period! He probably feels like locking you in your room and keeping his little girl forever. But he'll get over it, honey. Parents always do."

Judy put the long box containing the wedding dress into the back of her parents' car and hopped into the front seat. "Mother, will you drop me off at the train station?" she said on impulse. "I want to go see Russell."

Like many young Kansans living in small towns in the '50s, Russell was working a job 30 miles down the road in the next town.

"Oh. Don't you want to tell your father about the dress?" said her mother.

Judy shrugged. "That's okay. You can tell him."

When she got off the return train later that evening, Mrs. Myers was standing on the platform, her face tense, her mouth a tight line.

"Mother?" Judy said uncertainly. "What is it?"

"When I told your father we'd bought your wedding dress he — " Mrs. Myers stopped.

Judy's heart went cold. "He what?"

"He . . . had some sort of attack. He's paralyzed."

Judy felt paralyzed herself as she tried

to comprehend what the doctor was saying the next day at the hospital. *Fully paralyzed? But . . . why? Why?*

"We can't be sure," the doctor was saying, "but our initial diagnosis leans toward possible multiple sclerosis."

"B-but he's had no other symptoms," stammered Mrs. Myers.

"These things are always a shock," said the doctor. "We'll keep you informed as best we can. Right now, there's nothing you can do. You better go home and get some rest."

Judy sat silently in the car as her mother drove home. Her eyes were dry; she didn't feel like crying. In fact, she didn't feel anything at all . . . just kind of numb and cold, like a block of ice.

It took days to put words around the terrible, nagging feeling inside.

"Don't be silly. Of course it's not your fault!" Russell snapped when she tried to explain how she felt. "You can't blame yourself. These things just happen! I feel bad about your dad, too . . . but we've got to just keep going ahead."

After two weeks in the hospital, Judy's father had sufficiently improved to come home, but he still had no feeling in his hands and was not able to return to his work as a mechanic. The wedding plans stayed on schedule, but Judy had shifted into neutral. The excitement of getting married seemed to have gotten lost, and she couldn't find it again. And even though she was glad her father was better, she felt closed up and shut down when she was around him.

So she was surprised by the strange stirring she felt when she realized a man in the small office where she worked often caught her eye and smiled. It was the way a lot of men looked at her, ever since she could remember. She must be flirting with the man without knowing it, she chided herself. She was engaged, after all!

But . . . she had to admit she enjoyed the attention. He was older than she . . . he must think her very mature to be interested in her. Maybe there was nothing wrong with it; an innocent office friendship. . . .

But one day the hand that often rested on her shoulder as the man leaned over her desk discussing work to be done slid into her summer blouse, caressing her bare skin. It was an intimate moment, charged with secret excitement . . . so when he whispered, "Stay after work, okay?" it almost seemed inevitable what would happen next.

Russell felt like someone had just plunged a knife into his chest. He couldn't believe Judy was telling him this!

"Russell . . . say something!" Judy pleaded.

He just stared at her, uncomprehending, unbelieving.

She lowered her head. "You have every right to call off our engagement," she whispered. "I'll understand."

"Is that what you want?" Russell shot back.

"No, but — "

"Don't you love me any more?"

"Yes, I do love you, but — "

"Do you love this . . ." the word *creep* came to mind, ". . . guy?"

Judy shook her head. "No."

"Then *why*, for God's sake?!" Russell cried, his gut twisting so hard he thought he might throw up.

Judy kept shaking her head. "I don't know! Oh, Russell . . . I'm so sorry. What are we — what are you going to do?"

This time Russell shook his head. "I dunno," he said dully. "I can't think right now."

But for the next few days, Russell could think of nothing else. He and Judy had begun dating in high school. From their first date, he knew there was something special about this girl. "I was a lonely, unemotional sort of guy," Russell says about himself when he shares their story. "I couldn't believe that someone as special as Judy would pay any attention to me. She seemed older and wiser than the other girls, in a class by herself. What I didn't know then," he adds, "was how severely that specialness was going to be tested . . . or how that specialness would help sustain our marriage through some very painful years."

The two young people got engaged soon after high school graduation. "I thought everything was hunky-dory," Russell says. "Only later did I discover that shortly after we set our wedding date, Judy started an affair with this guy at her office. Looking back on it, the illness of her father seemed to precipitate it. She was acting very strange, very distant. When she finally told me about the affair, I was devastated. I felt betrayed . . . as though someone had taken something precious from me when I wasn't looking."

After several days of tearful and angry consideration, Russell and Judy decided to go ahead with their wedding as planned. "I managed to gain some semblance of control," Russell says, "rationalizing that Judy's affair was an isolated incident . . . that she was vulnerable because of her father's sudden illness. In order to do that, though, I pushed all the anger and pain I was feeling deep inside, not realizing I was turning off part of my being. I shut down what little emotional life I had, and unconsciously vowed that no one would ever hurt me this way again."

A small ironic smile plays on Russell's craggy face. "I was even kinda proud of myself for gritting my teeth and not succumbing to the expected male reaction of the time — this was the 1950s, remember — which would have been to walk away from Judy and feel justified . . . you know, the 'she done me wrong' song."

In the meantime, Judy was going through her own hell. "I felt so guilty," she says. "All my growing up years I'd felt like I had some magical power over boys. Older children and even adult males tended to relate to me in a sexual way. In some ways I didn't know how to play like other children. I felt like a 'woman/child' in a little girl's body. Whenever there was a sexual incident, I immediately assumed I'd done something to cause it to happen . . . which made me feel guilty and believe I was a bad person."

But the affair just before her wedding shocked her. "How could I have done such a thing? The shame was so great. I knew I had to tell Russell before our wedding day and allow him to get out of the engagement . . . I was astounded that, even after I told him, he still wanted us to get married."

August 4, 1956. The wedding day. The Episcopal church was bursting with flowers befitting such a joyous occasion. But as Judy walked down the aisle in her fairy-tale wedding dress on her father's arm — improved enough to give his daughter away, but unsteady on his feet — she still felt numb . . . and guilty. She knew their marriage could be declared null and void if the facts were made public to the church officials. But right after she and Russell exchanged their vows, an incredible feeling of relief washed over her. *Now I'm safe!* she thought. *I'm a married woman. Other men will leave me alone now . . . and if they don't, my husband will protect me.*

Wedding expectations run high. Much of the focus on flowers, dresses, and the ceremony are driven by a desire to create the perfect moment. We want the wedding to signal a marriage that is getting off to the right start.

The good news is that the wedding's purpose is to publicly place the couple's relationship in the hands of God. The bad news is that wedding fantasies do little to deal with the realities of relational life. In fact, the dynamics that face Judy and Russell have long histories predating their relationship. Thoughts and feelings which influence their actions are surrounded in mystery.

The whys of their thoughts and actions will take a lifetime to sort out. The father's illness and the affair both attempt to shatter the wedding fairyland. But denial wins out. Life goes on. Warm, safe, excited feelings of love fuel magical thinking. The days before Judy and Russell's wedding were more dramatic than most, but their story is a good reminder that every marriage starts with ignorance, imperfection, and idealism — for that is the nature of human relationships.

The newlyweds rented an apartment in the same small Kansas town where they'd gone to high school, and Russell attended the local junior college, working on his associate accounting degree. Ten months later, Judy gave birth to a healthy baby boy. Getting married *had* given her a feeling of safety, and now she had a new sense of responsibility.

"How I loved that little guy!" Judy says of baby Dillon. "I threw myself into being a mother. But," she admits, "I didn't know how to throw myself into being a wife. In a way I was still numb. Emotionally, I had little to give Russell."

Not that anything specific was wrong. Young and idealistic, Russell and Judy settled down to a life they hoped would be "happily ever after." They got involved in the local Episcopal church, he volunteered with the Junior Chamber of Commerce, and both had a lot of friends. "All of which," Russell concedes, "buffered our having to deal with each other."

As he recalls those early days of marriage, Russell leans forward intently, resting his elbows on the table — a good-looking man even in his sixties. "Judy became pregnant shortly after we were married," he recalls. "It was not a joint decision. She felt that children would solidify our marriage. I felt that I was too young to be married, let alone a father! After all, I was 20 years old, and Judy was 19. I thought we should become more stable before starting a family."

Like many young families, the Warner's financial condition was precarious. Neither Russell nor Judy had a college degree; then Judy became pregnant right away, so she quit work to care for their new little one. Even more stressful, little Dillon was sick almost from birth, and soon medical bills were added to their already overburdened financial resources.

"Still," Russell acknowledges, "Judy was right in one way. We both loved that little boy, and he did seem to add a stabilizing factor to our marriage. We focused most of our interactions around the baby and his needs."

Two years passed, and little Jacob joined the family. Then . . . a miscarriage.

"Oh, how I grieved for the child that would never be," Judy recalls. "I cried for days. Russell didn't understand my tears or the fact that I couldn't talk to him about it. He'd ask what was wrong, and I'd just shake my head. But the silence between us had been slowly growing, sort of like concrete forms that rise in preparation for building a great wall. I didn't know how to express what I felt, and I didn't know if he really wanted to hear or just wanted me to stop crying . . . so I said nothing."

Complicating her grief, Judy's father had never returned to work and still struggled with paralysis. In 1961, five years after the first onset of paralysis, he had a relapse and had to go into a nursing home. "Year after year I watched my father dying," Judy says, "but since I still felt responsible for his condition, I couldn't talk about that either! I wasn't able to verbalize what was happening then, but my feelings of isolation were like a casing of ice growing thicker and thicker around my emotions, and the wall between Russell and me grew higher and higher."

The next year, Judy became pregnant again. "With a third child on the way," Russell says, "I began to feel desperate to improve our financial situation. We'd been married six years by then; I'd gotten my associate degree, but accounting jobs in our small town were scarce. I was ready to try something new."

A management training opportunity for Russell in Wichita seemed to provide the hoped for "new beginning." The Warners packed up the boys and their belongings, said goodbye to their close-knit community of friends and family, and headed for the big city an hour away. A month later, Sarah was born — a little sister for Dillon and Jacob.

"Both Russell and I were delighted with our baby daughter," says Judy. "It seemed we knew how to be parents together . . . unfortunately, we didn't know how to be a married couple, didn't know how to talk to each other." Judy shakes her head sadly. "All that silence!"

Life demands and activities can keep us busy. Full days and tired nights run weeks into months. Time passes. Patterns are set. Years go by. Without communication, resources are drained. The renewing power of support and understanding shut down.

Unresolved issues of the past, compounded by emotional exhaustion, set couples up for disaster. We can only "look" good for so long. Parenting, working, and community life have their own joys and demands. But, it is the marital relationship in which the emotional stakes are the highest. The opportunity for intimacy sets the stage for both the highest demands and the greatest emotional rewards. Judy and Russell are driving along life's highway, but listening to their story one gets the feeling that repairs aren't getting made and the gas tank isn't being filled.

Unfortunately for the Warners, Russell's management training opportunity was abruptly withdrawn after a year, forcing him to take a sales job in the same company with a reduction in pay. Coupled with their lack of money management skills, their financial condition was once more in shambles.

"When the baby was only a year old, it looked like Judy would have to go to work in order to make ends meet," Russell says. "I couldn't admit it, but I was beginning to feel like a failure as a husband and provider. But it wasn't something Judy and I could talk about. We were not communicating!" Russell shakes his head ruefully. "Even our sex life was almost nonexistent."

For Russell, the walls of despair were growing thicker and higher. "Not knowing what else to do," he shrugs, "I just withdrew farther and farther into my world of silent anger and loneliness."

After six years of being "just Mommy," Judy reluctantly went back to work. "Each day I got dressed up, sadly dropped off the kids at a sitter's, and went out to the 'other world,' " she says. "On the job, however, I found my attractive, smiling face was noticed by attractive, smiling men. It triggered something inside, a familiar feeling of getting on a train which was barreling down a track at 500 miles an hour. I felt driven, like I had blinders on, so I couldn't look to the right or to the left."

One of the attractive, smiling men reminded her of her father. "Strangely, it was this man I was most attracted to," she says. "We began to have an affair — meeting after work or whenever I could come up with an excuse to get out of the house. But I was a basket-case of mixed emotions — intensely attracted to this man, confused because he reminded me of my father, afraid of being found out, desperately lonely and hungry for attention, angry at myself for cheating on Russell. *Why?* I kept asking myself. *Why am I doing this?*"

It didn't take Russell long to realize that "something" was going on. "The first affair just before our wedding took me completely by surprise," he says. "But not this time. The difference was that it wasn't very secretive. Oh, Judy made excuses about working over-time, late meetings, or church obligations . . . but I knew better." He winces, remembering. "I cannot adequately describe how I felt when she left the house for these 'meetings.' I tried to feel nothing . . . in fact, I refused to react at all, at least outwardly. But I was crying out inside. I wanted to scream; I wanted to smash things. I wanted to catch Judy and whoever this man was and take out all my fury, anger, and hatred on both of them."

As Russell and Judy tell this part of the story, they exchange glances. Russell shrugs. "Instead, I sat at home night after night, appearing — at least to Judy — that I did not care enough about our marriage, or her, to stop her. It was as though I was encased in ice, paralyzed and dying a very slow, agonizing death, incapable of reacting, even when I suspected — no, I *knew* — my wife was having an affair."

The affair at the office went on for several months. "But I couldn't handle the guilt and shame," Judy says, "especially when I looked in the eyes of my three children. In order to survive, I tried to separate myself into parts. I was living two lives: one as a good mother, committed to my family, attending church; and then, this other person, driven to attach myself to another man in a dependent relationship that involved sex, crying out to be taken care of."

Finally, unable to cope with living a double life, Judy went to the Episcopal priest and confessed, begging for help. The priest immediately referred both Judy and Russell to a psychiatrist at a Christian counseling center for help.

"Whoa, boy, I was really negative about *that*!" Russell says. "Seeking help from a psychiatrist was contrary to everything I believed in. I'd been taught that a man was expected to solve his own problems. Not only that, but going to a counselor meant admitting that there *was* a problem. What if our friends and family found out we were seeing somebody?"

Reluctantly, Russell agreed to a session

or two. "It wasn't as bad as I thought," Russell says. "After all, Judy admitted being the one with the problem, and the doctor seemed to agree with her, relieving me of any responsibility for the condition of our marriage . . . or so I thought. I would only go to the sessions when it was convenient, and then I would sit with my arms folded across my chest, refusing to become an active participant."

During this period of time, first Judy's father, then her mother, died within a year of each other. He'd been paralyzed for 10 years. *Why don't I cry?* Judy wondered. *Why do I still feel so numb?*

As the therapy sessions continued, however, it seemed to Russell that Judy was getting better. She appeared more peaceful and relaxed. She was even beginning to smile and have fun.

It made him feel resentful. "I still felt lonely and angry," he says. "It was like she was getting better . . . but our marriage was not. The only area of life that made me happy was our children. In fact, in 1968 we welcomed our fourth child — another daughter we named Cara. By this time, Dillon was eleven, Jacob was nine, and Sarah six. We had a great time together! It seemed I knew how to be a good father, even though I did not know how to be a good husband."

Life-draining patterns get "fixes." Some are quick and superficial, others are real and meaningful. Judy turns to affairs first, then to counseling. Work and kids define Russell's world.

Being a good wife and being a good husband requires self-awareness and self-expression on the one hand, and open, caring support on the other. Tough tasks anytime . . . but especially tough in the midst of all the issues Russell and Judy were experiencing.

The January wind was howling around the Warner's cozy three-bedroom bungalow in a pleasant Wichita suburb. The New Year had just ushered in 1970 — a new year, a new decade, a time for new beginnings.

But as Judy sat on the couch listening to the storm outside, the bitter wind seemed to clutch her spirit with its icy fingers and drop her outside. Russell was working late; the children were just a few feet away from her absorbed in a TV show. But she felt so isolated . . . so distant from all of them.

As the familiar loneliness welled up inside, she shivered, as if she were outside, alone in the storm, walking down the snow-covered sidewalk at dusk looking in the windows of people's houses. She saw lights, and warmth, and laughter inside . . . but she was outside, looking in, her nose pressed against the window. As she imagined other people's happiness and togetherness, a terrible longing gripped her. She wanted it so much! Instead, she was alone, and empty.

As she sat numbly on the couch, another feeling pushed its way into her consciousness. Loathing . . . of herself. In spite of the years of helpful counseling, the old compulsive feelings that had driven her before to attach herself to an aggressive, demanding man were gathering their power over her once more. On the verge of another affair, she felt like the Lorelei, the mythical Germanic siren, whose singing out in the ocean lured the Rhine river boatmen to destruction on a reef.

She hated herself. She was no better than a Siren, destroying the people around her. But she felt powerless to stop what was happening.

Watching her children, Judy felt overwhelmed by guilt and pain. *I love them so much,* she thought. *But I'm hurting them too much to go on living.* To dull the ache, she got up, went into the kitchen, and poured herself a straight shot of bourbon whiskey to wash down a Valium. Then she went back into the living room, pried the kids away from the TV, and put the younger ones to bed. Another shot of whiskey . . . another pill. . . .

By the time all the kids were in bed, Judy had lost count of how many shots of bourbon and how many pills she had taken. But instead of taking away the pain, her loneliness had intensified. Shakily, she called her priest, then her psychiatrist, then Russell. "I just don't care any more," she told them.

No one really heard her cry for help. "You're drunk," Russell told her in disgust.

"Go to bed and sleep it off," the psychiatrist said.

She crawled into bed, not caring whether she ever woke up again.

Sunlight streamed into her bedroom window the next morning. The wind had died down. Judy opened her eyes, glad to see the winter sunshine . . . and then it hit her.

I tried to kill myself last night! she thought, horrified. Getting gingerly out of bed, trying to not jostle the stabbing hangover she had, she heard Cara noisily banging the side of her crib, wanting out. After changing Cara's soaking diaper, Judy hurried into the kitchen with the toddler on her hip. Russell was tossing down a cup of coffee, talking to Dillon about basketball, and

Jacob and Sarah were fighting for the plastic prize in a box of cold cereal.

It was all so chaotic and . . . normal.

Shaken by the realization that she could be dead by now, Judy somehow mumbled goodbye to Russell and got the kids off to school as if in a trance . . . then got down on her knees by the living room couch.

"Oh, God," she prayed . . . and then stopped. *What have I done?* she thought desperately. *Will God even hear me?*

"Oh, God," she started again, tears streaming down her cheeks, "if you're anywhere around, Sir, I sure could use Your help. I don't know what to do, but . . . I-I can't live this way any longer. I'm either going to stay sick . . . or get well . . . either way, it isn't up to me any longer. I want You to be in charge."

Great gulping sobs wracked Judy's body as she knelt by the couch. She cried and cried . . . and when it seemed as if she had no tears left, she whispered the General Confession of the Episcopal Church and then the Lord's Prayer.

Our Father, Who art in heaven,
Hallowed be Thy Name.
Thy kingdom come, Thy will be done
On earth, as it is in heaven. . . .

Remembering that pivotal day, Judy now says, "As I cried out in desperation, Jesus came into the room, and it was like He took loads and loads of luggage out of my arms that I couldn't carry. He released the weights that were fastened to my ankles, pulling me into the whirlpool of hell."

After she finished crying, Judy got up. She sensed something important had happened to her.

Timid about having such a profound "conversion" experience, Judy at first didn't tell anyone what had happened. But as time passed, she realized she was beginning to feel like a new person. The compulsion to have the affair was gone; she didn't go through with it. What freedom!

Judy describes some of the changes she was experiencing this way: "I'd be talking with Dillon about school or reading to Sarah, and suddenly realize I didn't feel guilty. I wasn't leading a double life any more. What my children saw is what they got — a mom who loved them and wanted to do what was best for them. I found myself really enjoying the kids, laughing more, and best of all, feeling peaceful inside. I thought, *Is this what feeling forgiven is all about?*"

But one thing hadn't changed much — her relationship with Russell. "I hadn't told him about my experience with the Lord in our living room," she admits, "because I didn't think he'd understand. I was afraid he'd think I was trying to minimize my behavior by saying I felt God had forgiven me. I tried to work on my marriage — getting help from my psychiatrist, reading self-help books, trying to use 'I' messages — but it was still hard to talk to him."

What Judy remembers most about Russell at this time was the way that he folded his arms across his chest, not allowing her to be physically or emotionally close to him. "He assumed this posture sitting in a chair, even in bed," she says, shaking her head and imitating the stoic, Indian-chief position. "For me, it was a figure of judgment. I found it almost impossible to cross that barrier of silent criticism."

Russell admits that Judy's perceptions were pretty accurate. "I saw her growing personally, and my resentment deepened because it made my own condition seem even worse. From time to time she would ask me to read books or listen to tapes that had helped her, but I still didn't want to admit that I needed help. After all, the condition of our marriage was her fault, wasn't it? She pleaded with me to talk to her, but I refused; what was there to talk about? Besides, I was afraid that if we started talking, all my anger would come boiling out and . . . well, I might lose control. That was something I was always afraid of — losing control, getting violent. So I would hold myself rigidly in control, sitting defiantly with my arms folded. No way was I going to dig into my feelings. Judy would eventually give up and leave the room in tears."

"I just couldn't get through to him," Judy says. "I felt like I was yelling across a great chasm, but all I heard was the echo of my own voice. I kept asking myself, *Can't Russell see that I've changed?* I thought I was trying and he wasn't, so my feelings of frustration and loneliness just continued in a hopeless spiral. Frankly, I was tired; it felt like our relationship had run into a brick wall. What was the point of continuing?"

During this time, Judy continued meeting with the psychiatrist at the Christian counseling center, whether or not Russell came along. But one evening as the two of them left the doctor's office, Judy turned to Russell and said in a matter-of-fact voice, "Russell, either you accept your responsibility in our marriage, or it's over. I'm not going to live the rest of my life this way."

Russell was stunned. "She'd made threats before when she was upset," he recalls, "but somehow I knew this was different. She meant it."

As they drove home together in silence, Russell's insides were churning. Judy had never acted like this before! It was an ultimatum, delivered calmly but firmly. He panicked. Had he made his ego more important than his marriage? Why wasn't he willing to look at his responsibility for what was wrong with their marriage? He had to admit that Judy had changed . . . a lot. But their relationship was still a shambles.

"For the first time," Russell says, "I had to admit to myself that maybe, just maybe, our marital problems weren't *just* the extramarital affairs, and Judy wasn't the only one at fault."

With that, Russell's icy exterior began to crumble.

A healthy marriage always takes two. Personal health options abound; each of us always have room for individual growth. But sooner or later, relationships can only go as far as both participants are willing to go together.

Life together creates a two-edged sword. A spouse can love and affirm in ways that are unavailable in any other relationship. A spouse can also call to our attention our shortcomings and immaturity like no other person.

Emotional walls began to fall for Russell and Judy. A scary and exciting journey into marital reconciliation and personal growth began. With this, unified hope could also begin.

To Judy's amazement, Russell took her confrontive words at the doctor's office seriously.

"With the psychiatrist's help, I began to look at my part of the problem in our marriage," Russell says. "I realized I wasn't working very hard to bridge the gap that was keeping us apart. Frankly, I hadn't really tried to understand Judy or to listen to what she had to say. I had been so caught up keeping myself together, keeping a tough exterior, trying to manage the stresses of my job, our finances, and our marriage on my own, that I wasn't letting Judy into my life. I didn't dare make myself vulnerable."

As Russell looked at his own part of the marriage, he began to have a new respect for Judy. "I marveled at her fortitude in working hard at putting her own life together, as well as working on our relationship. She was working outside the home, maintaining a household, and trying to be the mother our children needed — all without much moral support from me. It had been hard to give her that support because, frankly, I still felt guilty about her having to work outside the home. It was painful to admit to myself, much less anyone else, that I felt like a failure as a husband and a provider."

Russell faced the reality that maybe he couldn't handle everything by himself. "For the first time in my life," he says, "I considered the possibility that I needed to ask for help — not only from Judy and from others, but from God."

As Russell began to admit some of his feelings, the Warner marriage moved out of its numbing silence — but now he and Judy began having angry, bitter fights, each blaming the other for hurt feelings and wrongs suffered.

At a friend's suggestion, they signed up for a Marriage Encounter weekend. "We'd been married 19 years by then — 1975 — but that weekend really opened our eyes to a new way of communicating with each other," Judy says. "We learned how to examine our feelings and write about them individually, then sharing what we'd written with each other and talking about it. We also learned that there are other things to say to each other besides hurtful, angry thoughts."

A high point of the weekend for Judy was hearing the story of *The Man of LaMancha*. Don Quixote loved Aldonza the whore, whose "father" was a regiment passing by, and who had been born in a ditch. "Their story became a picture of what my life had been like," Judy says. "When I heard Aldonza sing the sad song of her life, all my feelings of shame and guilt came pouring out in tears. I had felt like a regiment of men had passed through my life for so long, leaving me lying in a ditch. As I listened to the words and music of compassion and forgiveness pouring out through Don Quixote's love for Aldonza, transforming her into Dulcinea, Don Quixote's lady, I began believing that Russell and I could be transformed into each other's lord and lady. For the first time, I truly believed our marriage could be changed."

The Marriage Encounter weekend had a similar effect on Russell. "Learning new ways to communicate began breaking down some of the high walls of separation that I had experienced," he says. "As we began communicating more effectively, I, too, began to see hope for our marriage. I had always talked more about the weather, football scores, and the latest political situation than I had about my own feelings. For the first time I was able to talk about some of my desires, hurts, and joys with Judy. I was amazed at the level of intimacy this created between us."

The other side of sharing feelings, they learned, is listening. "As Judy shared some of her desires, hurts, and joys with me, I began to see a lonely little girl — not the independent, strong woman she hid behind. I was finally learning that what Judy wanted most was a caring, loving husband, someone to love her, care for her, and protect her."

Russell looks appreciatively at Judy, still an attractive woman in her fifties. "I also began to see my wife in yet another light. The gifts of compassion and love she brought to our marriage were very special qualities that had helped sustain us through many years of agony. I also began to see her spirituality, which had been masked for so long."

An overnight transformation? Hardly. "It wasn't easy communicating at a deep level for a man out of touch with his emotions for 20 years," Russell confesses. "Even though I was beginning to come out from behind the walls I'd built up around myself, I still kept the option open to retreat behind them if I felt too threatened."

One incident stands out which helped

Russell see what he was doing. "For instance," Russell continues, "one evening we were having quite an argument. Judy was being very confrontive about some issues I needed to deal with in our marriage; I thought that was pretty high and mighty of her, given what she'd done to our marriage, so I said, 'That's it; I'm leaving!' " He grabbed the car keys and stormed out the door. His intention was to spend the night at his office and really worry Judy.

But as he drove down the street, he quickly discovered two things: one, there was no gas in the car; two, he had no money with him. His running away was short-lived. He parked in a nearby supermarket parking lot until the call of nature forced him to return home — rather sheepishly.

"Although that incident was pretty humorous even then," Russell admits with a grin, "it showed me that the very thing Judy was confronting me about — my tendency to avoid my responsibility for things that go wrong — was something I had to deal with."

For Russell, one of the major things he had to deal with was some unfinished business. "I realized that before I could become that caring, loving husband Judy desired, *I had to forgive her* for all those years of pain and anguish I had lived through because of the affairs. It was one of the hardest things I have ever had to do," he says honestly. "Giving up my resentment and anger and bitterness was like giving up an old friend. I felt entitled to my anger, and I especially did not want to let Judy 'off the hook.'"

But as Russell wrestled with what forgiveness involved, he realized something else: he needed to ask Judy to forgive *him* for his part in their struggle for so many years.

"When Russell asked for my forgiveness," Judy says, "it uncovered a deep well of my own anger and bitterness toward him that I had no idea was there. I had to work hard to forgive him for distancing himself from me, for the many years of silence and loneliness and isolation."

Nor did forgiveness happen in one fell swoop. It was a slow, painful process, punctuated by some heavy fighting and blaming of each other.

"But in the midst of the process, we were using some of our new communication skills and listening to each other," Russell says. "We discovered that much of our fighting was actually a power struggle going on between us. I have a strong, competitive drive, and I always want to win at arguments, games . . . everything. I kept trying to beat

Judy down, so that I would come out on top. But eventually I began to see that winning wasn't everything. When I took the time to really listen to what Judy was trying to say to me, we both ended up winning."

Learning, growing, striving for a healthy relationship is hard work. No fairy tales and fantasies now. Judy and Russell are now building this marriage on rock-solid reality.

Open expressions replace closed isolation. Honesty replaces denial, and forgiveness replaces blame. New tools for old problems. Skills for the task. Energy for the effort. Layer by layer the dead and dirty is washed away. New life is reborn.

The Warner family was growing up — in more ways than one. The three older children married and were on their own. In 1981 Judy and Russell had celebrated their silver anniversary — 25 years! A few years later Cara, the youngest, started college.

And then darkness closed in once more. Russell slid into a depressed state "that I can only describe as a mid-life crisis," he says. "Part of it was the marriage relationship. Every time I thought we were making headway, something else came up to work on. Sometimes I felt like screaming, 'When does it end?' "

But there were other things, too. Several
years earlier, Russell had felt stuck in a dead-
end job. Even when he changed jobs, he felt
like he did nothing but work, sleep, work,
sleep. "I'd come home tired from work and
go to sleep, just to wake up in the morning
and go to work again," he says. "I wasn't
going anywhere, just 'round and 'round in a
big, dark pit. Life wasn't much fun."

The many years of feeling closed, lonely,
and angry resurfaced, and once more Russell
sank into silence. His and Judy's sex life,
which had often been a barometer of how
well their relationship was doing, became
almost nonexistent.

"This added to my depression," Russell
remembers. "Once again we were living
separate lives. Judy and I had weathered so
many storms together, our kids were grown
and out of the nest — the time for us was
here! Instead, we were talking about divorce
. . . when we were talking at all. I felt caught
in a trap again and didn't know how to get
out."

At first Russell's depression and the silence between them was subtle — until Judy
recognized the old loneliness boiling up
within her again. She felt at a loss for what
to do. The words of Neil Diamond's popu-

lar song (sung by Barbra Streisand) haunted her.

> You don't send me flowers,
> You don't sing me love songs anymore.
> And you'd think I could learn
> How to tell you goodbye.

Why can't I learn how to tell Russell goodbye and just get on with my life? she thought.

As the distance between Judy and Russell widened, she once again began thinking about a divorce. She also developed a deepening friendship with a man she'd known for many years. It felt so good to have someone to talk to, someone to care about her. But she was scared. The old compulsive feelings were welling up inside once more; she felt like she was losing control.

"After all those years," Judy says, "I was again on the verge of an affair. I put on the brakes, but soon there was another male friend. Russell was shut up in his own world and not very aware (I thought) of what was happening with me." Again Judy ended the relationship, but then a third man stepped into the void.

"I was so frightened that I was getting my needs met outside my marriage with these non-sexual affairs," Judy says. A friend suggested she change the kind of job she had so she wouldn't have to deal with men. Judy got out of the office and into the classroom as a Head Start teacher. "I also purposefully gained weight, and started dressing drably so I wouldn't be attractive," she says.

But she also did something even more important. "I knew something was going on with me at a deep level. Even though I was frightened, I found the courage to go back to therapy to get some answers."

This time the therapist probed Judy's earliest memories of her relationships with the opposite sex — including her father. Gradually she recalled sleeping often in the same bed with him as a child. He had lavished affection and attention on her, they shared secrets and confidences — a twosome which often shut her mother out. At age 12 . . . a wall went up in Judy's memory.

Gradually the truth came out. At age 12, Judy's father had sexually assaulted her. But before that, she had suffered emotional incest from him, placed in the position of "surrogate wife." He lavished affection, time, and attention on Judy which rightfully belonged to her mother.

"I was in shock!" Judy confesses. "I had buried all this in my unconsciousness, and at age 12 started living a lie, keeping this secret even from myself. Now all my defenses, secrets, and lies were out. I felt like someone coming out of a basement after a tornado had destroyed everything I owned, stunned, surveying the damage. But once the shock wore off, I had to sort out my life and determine what was salvageable and what was gone forever."

Learning about the incest was a revelation for Russell. "*Finally* some things began making sense to me," he says. "I began to understand why Judy was driven to have affairs with other men, especially men who reminded her of her father. She was acting out the sexual and emotional abuse she'd experienced as a child; it was like an ingrained part of her life, even though it had been buried in her subconscious. I also began to understand this was not something I could have prevented, even if I had been different."

One of the things that had been hard for Russell to understand was *why* Judy needed so much protection. "She'd always seemed like a person who was very sure of herself, getting what she wanted. I didn't understand why she needed to be taken care of."

Children find a way of coping. Sometimes they are forced to handle incredible dysfunction and trauma. Such is the case of sexual abuse. A child should never be condemned regarding "how" they manage under the stress of abuse. Children do the best they can. When the challenges are overwhelming, children customize strategies which help them survive. However, these strategies are limited and set in motion major handicaps for healthy emotional development.

Incest is one of the most powerful of childhood traumas. Children do not have the capacity to understand a parent's sexual dysfunction and the pathology of their parents' marriage. A child cannot say, "My father has a problem." A child can only blame him or herself or deny that anything bad is happening. The sin of incest turns a child's world upside-down. The safe world of a parent's affection and encouragement is twisted into a dangerous place.

Survivors of incest have a long, hard road to emotional well-being. Uncovering the layers of shut down feelings and childhood coping strategies takes time and support. Anger at one parent, then the other parent, then of God and the world in general are common. Both the abuse itself and the lack of protection make for complicated emotional healing. Ambivalence about trusting, being helped, and self-image abound. Sexual mixed feelings and overall fears of intimacy put incredible strains on marriage. Most incest survivors need an individually guided process. Spouses also must find a way to gain the understanding and learn the responses they need to be helpful.

Russell was asked by Judy to join her as she took the First Step of a Twelve Step Program for Sexual Addiction. "As I listened to Judy working through the First Step, in which a person admits being powerless over their addiction and that their life had become unmanageable, and then identifies examples of the emotional and physical abuse, many things became clear to me that I simply had not understood before. Judy had never been allowed to be 'just a little girl.' She had lost so much of her childhood and suffered so much she was not ready for, emotionally and physically. The need to be taken care of so much was a result of not being taken care of and protected as a child. The person who should have protected her — her father — was the perpetrator. This left a deep void in her life, a desperate need she was always looking for."

Besides the Twelve Step program, Judy also began attending an incest survivor's group and started reading a lot about dysfunctional family issues. Because all of this was taking a long time for her to work through, she decided to put the decision about whether she and Russell should get a divorce on hold. "So much was going on," she says, "I knew I wasn't ready to make a good decision about that."

The return of old destructive patterns is devastating. "When will it ever end?" is a common plea. Demoralizing as times of trouble are, they do set in motion the chance to go deeper into the issues of our lives. Sometimes our partner helps, sometimes he or she can't.

Couples may mistake dry spells in marital life as cause for divorce. Like Judy and Russell, they are most often signals of further needs to be addressed. Being emotionally distant at times in married life is normal. Rather than blame, use the time for personal examination. Not feeling in love is important to share, but doesn't need to be legally acted upon. Both Russell and Judy needed all of their emotional strength to cope with their own issues. As they re-established themselves individually, the ability to be emotionally in the marriage came back.

The discovery in 1985 that Judy was a

victim of incest was "like a spring rain washing away the winter dirt and debris," Russell says. "But even though I had new knowledge, my own wounds were still there. I still experienced a lot of anger and pain. I also knew that *my* way of coping with the anger was to be silent, and in the past I had used that silence like a weapon."

Russell went back for therapy at the Christian counseling center to help him over the rough places. As the therapy progressed, he also began coming out of the depression which had created so much darkness for him. Besides his own issues, he was also learning how to live with an incest survivor.

"At best, it's difficult," he admits. "But Judy's therapy was helping her immensely, and this in turn made it easier for us to recover together."

Once again Russell and Judy were communicating. They also made a priority of spending time alone together on the weekends and took some important vacations away from home, just to be together and focus on enjoying each other.

"All of this has taken a very long time," Judy agrees. "I've been in therapy for several years and have come to know at a very deep level just how badly I was injured both emotionally and sexually as a child — and *how much* that has affected me as an adult. I have come to understand the loneliness that has haunted me for so long, hiding a secret I didn't even dare tell myself."

In addition, Judy has had to work through a massive layer of anger, betrayal, and grief. She has had to mourn her lost childhood, and the lost years of a happy marriage. "I really don't know when all the mourning will stop," she says even now, "but I know it will stop eventually. I'll know it's over when it's over."

Most hopefully, positive, healing steps have begun. "I'm learning to love myself, take care of myself, and to be a friend to others along the way," Judy says. "In addition, I've become less demanding in my relationship with Russell. As I've understood my own needs that weren't met as a child, I've also understood that Russell can't be everything for me. I've built up a support group of friends to call on so the complete burden isn't on my husband. When I start feeling scared about being a sex addict and think I might not be able to control it, I make a phone call to a Twelve Step friend or to my therapist."

Part of dealing with an addiction is to realize one is always an addict. Judy says it's important for work the Twelve Step program daily — "whether I want to or not. But it's worth it," she says. "Working my program means staying sexually sober — and that means continued freedom for me from the addiction that literally could have killed me."

Another part of dealing with an addiction, Judy says, is establishing boundaries for herself. "I realize now that I over-trusted people. I should have been able to trust my father, but he abused that trust. I also over-trusted the other men in my life because I was so desperate to be loved and cared for. Also, because my abuse happened as a child, I didn't know how to set boundaries. Those two things — over-trust and lack of boundaries — allowed me to be victimized many times."

Some of the boundaries Judy has developed include:

1. Be honest with myself and with others.

2. Don't keep any secrets from Russell; keep him current on what I'm thinking and feeling.

3. Don't have any secrets from my therapist.

4. Don't create a separate, hidden life for myself apart from Russell.

5. Recognize rituals that lead to unwanted behaviors, and then get out of them if they start.

6. Call a friend if I'm feeling scared.

It was also immensely helpful, Judy says, when she decided to go back to school. "Going to school to get my degree helped change my focus. I'm not just trying to survive or hang on; now I have a goal to work for. As I see myself passing the milestones toward that goal, I feel a great sense of satisfaction and accomplishment. I feel good about myself. I'm becoming a new person with new skills and things I can contribute to others."

All strong marriages build structures and patterns into their relationships that work for them. Many of these ways of functioning are similar to all couples. Trust, open communication, conflict resolution, understanding, and caring are a few standards. Couples also customize their patterns of relating to fit their individual needs and history.

Over the years we learn each other's emotional soft spots. The vulnerability needed for intimacy also provides the ammunition for a deadly assault if not handled carefully. Healthy guidelines help couples to manage their marriage. Positive routines build marital stability. With each partner focused on taking responsibility for his or her own life, a freedom can build in the marriage. Each spouse works to give all they can and to accept whatever their partner is able to give. The result is a relationship freely given, thankfully received, in harmony with God's grace.

Six years after learning about the incest, Russell and Judy faced another brief but important crisis. Judy strongly felt the need to continue in therapy; Russell thought "enough was enough!" He wanted her to get out of therapy and get on with their lives, like "normal people."

A line was drawn in the sand; the possibility of divorce once again hung in the air.

Seeing how strongly Judy felt about it, Russell wisely came to the point of "taking hands off" the process. "His willingness to let me continue therapy was very important to me," Judy says. "It's true; I may never feel able to make it without support. But an even larger reality is that our chances of staying together — not to mention enjoying a *good* marriage — were almost nil. Yet both things are happening. We have not only stayed together for almost 40 years, but we are now enjoying the hard-won fruits of a good marriage! We fought odds that would have made many couples throw in the towel. But we didn't. We persevered."

After beating the odds, it's not likely that Russell and Judy will paint a plastic "happily ever after" veneer over their marriage. "There are still times when the old anger and pain boil up, and I get the urge to cut and run," Russell admits. "That's offset, however, by the reality that we still are *moving forward* together."

"It's a choice," Judy says simply. "I had to decide that I wanted my life to change; that I wanted to grow. But before I could do that, I had to learn the 'whys' — why my past kept getting in the way of my present; what the connections were between my childhood trauma and adult behavior."

"We are choosing to stay together," Russell agrees. "Through therapy we've learned how to change the destructive patterns that had become a habit, so that our 'dance of intimacy' could become less stiff and awkward, more smooth and flowing."

"Like when we used to go country-western dancing," Judy laughs. "At the beginning I had to dance backward all the time because Russell hadn't gotten the hang of it. Now Russell also takes his turn going backward, so that I can go forward. That's a very real example of what we're doing more often in our life together — taking turns, listening to each other more readily, using our new insights."

More soberly she adds, "There's a saying that 'love is a decision.' I have to decide to love each day whether I *feel* like it or not. I chose — still choose — to risk again with Russell, because Russell has also chosen to grow. He has risked letting me know about the pain and fears in his own life, and that's helped me understand the man who was so closed and hidden for so many years. What I see now is his kindness and goodness which has been freed from its prison of fear, resentment, and loneliness."

Like Don Quixote and Aldonza, Russell and Judy Warner choose to see past the grit of "reality" to the real person who is inside — and by that very choosing, help lift each other out of the prisons of their past and into the freedoms of their future.

Chapter Two
===

"Though He Slay Me, Yet Will I Trust Him"

Sunday afternoon, August 8, 1976, was hot and dry when Lorraine Evans finally started putting things back into their newly renovated bedroom. Slowly, room by room, they were redecorating the big, old house they'd purchased a few months earlier when they'd moved to this small Kansas town. It was like the process she and her husband, Bob, were going through in putting their lives back together after a painful separation, divorce, and remarriage. One "room" at a time, their lives were finally taking shape.

But on that afternoon, Lorraine was glad that Bob and all six of their kids were out of the house. It gave her a little time to think and work.

Bob, an over-the-road truck driver, had left earlier that morning for his Oklahoma run, and Tyler, their next-to-youngest, was playing with his cousins at Lorraine's sister's house. After church and Sunday dinner, the five other Evans children had gone swimming.

It was the custom in their new church with its large, active youth group for most of the kids to spend Sunday afternoon at the nearby Gridley municipal swimming pool. Then they would all trek back to church for the evening youth group. Since they had so many children, Lorraine usually drove her kids. But that Sunday afternoon, Rosemary, the Evans' neighbor a mile up the country road, had called and offered the use of her large station wagon. "Kenny's gonna drive," she said. "Is that okay with you?"

Kenny was the pastor's 17-year-old son and a responsible, good driver. Lorraine didn't hesitate to say yes.

A few minutes later, Kenny, with Rosemary's two girls, had wheeled the blue station wagon into the Evans' yard to pick up the happy quintet: Barbara, just fifteen; Ray, almost fourteen; Brent, twelve; Troy, nine; and seven-year-old Ruth.

With the kids off to the pool, Lorraine was deep into sorting pillowcases and old family photo albums, deciding what would go into the dresser and what would be stored in the closet, when the phone rang.

"Have the kids left your house yet?" said an anxious-sounding Rosemary.

"Sure. They left 10 or 15 minutes ago." There was silence on the other end of the line, so Lorraine prodded, "Why?"

"Well," said Rosemary in a spacey-sounding voice, "my sister-in-law just called and said there was a terrible train accident at Gridley in which some kids in a blue station wagon were killed. . . ." Her voice trailed off.

"Oh, Rosemary, don't worry," Lorraine reassured her neighbor in a take-charge way. "You know that wasn't your car. It's not our kids." Still Rosemary remained silent. "Hey, I'll tell you what," Lorraine continued, "how 'bout if I pop over and pick you up and we drive over to the pool — just to reassure ourselves? Okay?"

"Thanks, Lorraine —" and the phone quietly clicked dead.

Lorraine got in the car and was starting down their long driveway toward the country road that passed their house when off in the distance she saw a highway patrol car coming.

She caught her breath. The highway patrol worked the highways, not their little county road. *What is he doing? Could Rosemary be right?* she worried.

But the patrolman passed the Evans' driveway, and Lorraine regained her breath.

Slowly Lorraine turned onto the road and followed the patrol car . . . at a distance. She really didn't want to catch up, but up ahead the cruiser stopped in the middle of the two-lane road to talk to someone in an oncoming car.

When Lorraine pulled to a stop behind him, the woman in the oncoming car, another neighbor, pointed toward her. The patrolman turned around to look.

A nauseous feeling clutched Lorraine's stomach. The patrolman got out of his car and slowly adjusted his Smoky Bear hat. It took forever for him to walk the few yards back to her car.

Like a dream in which familiar people keep popping up in unexpected places, Lorraine realized that she knew the patrolman. He was a member of their church, and she had seen him that very morning.

But he didn't look at her. He wrung his hands and adjusted his hat again and stared off across the meadow. He cleared his throat. "Hi, Lorraine," he muttered.

"What's the problem? Is this some kind

of an inspection?" she asked calmly, ter-rified of his answer.

"Not really." He still hadn't looked at her. "It's, uh . . . more of a personal thing," he stumbled. He cleared his voice again and finally looked at her.

Below his mirrored, aviator-style sun-glasses his cheeks were streaked with wet-ness. Lorraine realized they were tears. *What could be breaking him up so badly?* Lorraine wondered vaguely.

Finally, the officer continued. "I, uh, I need to tell you that your kids have been in-volved in a terrible automobile accident." He cleared his throat again. "We sent one of your boys to the hospital."

Lorraine swallowed hard, trying to re-main calm. *One, only one. That was good, wasn't it?* "What about the rest of them? Are they okay?"

"I, uh . . . uh." The patrolman looked back up the road toward his cruiser. "Well, we sent one boy to the hospital," he drawled in a slow Kansas accent.

"But what about my girls? Tell me about my girls!"

His shoulders fell. "They're both gone," he mumbled.

"And the boys?" she rushed on, refus-ing to let the news register. "You said you sent only one to the hospital. Are the other two okay?"

"Uh, not really. Actually, there was only one boy alive to send to the hospital." The patrolman looked desperate. "You've got to get there yourself, Lorraine, real soon. I think the one we sent to the hospital was Troy. That's all I know."

Lorraine watched dumbfounded as the officer walked across the road. He stood with his back to her as he pulled out his handkerchief and wiped his eyes. When he came back he said, "I need the name of a funeral home — whichever one you want to use."

"Funeral home? I don't know any funeral homes around here. We only moved here eight months ago," she snapped. "Why do you need the name of a funeral home?"

"You need to select one."

"Why? What for?"

"Come on, Lorraine. Don't make this any harder than it is . . . for you or for me."

Lorraine stared blankly at him.

"Lorraine, some of your children . . . four of your children died in that crash with the train. We have to know where you want us to take their bodies."

Slowly the horror began to sink in. "How should I know where to take them?" she whispered numbly. "Never before have any of my children. . . ." She still couldn't say the word. "You choose. I don't care."

"I'm not allowed to make any suggestions."

How bizarre, thought Lorraine, her mind screaming in protest. *I don't want to do this! But he can't help me decide where to send the bodies of my children.* Finally she mumbled a name she recalled from another fatal automobile accident she'd read about in the newspaper.

The officer wrote it down and then said, "Why don't you follow me over to Rosemary's place and leave your car there, then I'll take both of you to the hospital."

After they had picked up Rosemary, they had to pass the accident site to get to the hospital, but the patrolman didn't want to stop. "Nothin' here for you to see," he said. "You need to get to the hospital." But Lorraine and Rosemary stared silently out the window at the bright orange tarp that nearly covered the mangled remains of Rosemary's blue station wagon.

"Are they still there?" Rosemary whispered in shock. She knew one of her daughters had also died in the crash — but she didn't know which one.

"Yes, ma'am. But now that you've told us where to take them, we'll see that they are removed as quickly as possible."

He flipped a switch. "Could you clear the way, please!" The voice of the patrolman blasted metallically over the bullhorn as he tried to weave his cruiser through the maze of onlookers and cars that lined both sides of the road. Lorraine hid her head, but somehow — even in the middle of the bright afternoon — the flashing red lights invaded the dark, air-conditioned cruiser.

Lorraine kept thinking that she was moving through a terrible dream and would wake up soon to find it wasn't true. Then she wouldn't have to tell Bob the horrible news.

It was not until they got to the hospital that the two women discovered for certain who was still alive. Only Troy and one of Rosemary's girls had been brought in. The other six children died in the car. They included Kenny, the pastor's son who had been driving, one of Rosemary's daughters, and four Evans children.

It took Lorraine 18 hours before she was able to contact her husband. That morning Bob had driven his personal car to the franchise food service warehouse in Kansas City, where he had loaded his truck and headed out on the road.

At his first stop in Tulsa, Oklahoma, on Monday morning the manager said that he had an emergency phone call.

When Bob called home and found out what had happened, he was devastated. He had always been the strong, silent type — a quality that had played a part in ruining their marriage once. But a lot had changed. He had learned how to be in touch with his feelings . . . and he knew he couldn't be strong for this; he couldn't hold up Lorraine.

"You're gonna have to find your own support somewhere else," he told his wife honestly when he finally got home. "I can't even handle it myself."

Few can imagine, even fewer have experienced first-hand this depth of devastating loss. Even relatively mild traumas throw couples into cycles of shock, anger, sorrow, and blame. No couple can prepare for the loss of a child.

Commonly, spouses develop patterns where one strives to be up when the other is down; hopeful when the other is discouraged; strong when the other is weak. When our worlds crash in with such overwhelming force, there is little either spouse can do. Like two chronically ill persons sharing a hospital room, their ability to help each other is minimal.

Crises draw some people together, bringing the best out of them. But, given the Evans' rough history, it was not at all certain that they could rise to the occasion.

Bob and Lorraine had met in high school. He remembers her as outgoing and involved in everything. In contrast, he was the rugged, quiet type. "Her magnetic personality turned me on," he says with a smile.

Today, sitting around their kitchen table telling their story, Lorraine meets Bob's smile and says, "I had dated quite a bit, but from the first day I saw Bob, I was attracted to him. And he's right that I was outgoing, but that was on the outside. Inside I was the most insecure introvert alive. I only acted as though I was outgoing because I had learned that was what people liked. Somehow in Bob's quietness, however, I sensed that he liked the real me. He went along with everything I ever wanted to do."

This mutual attraction kept them together even after high school. Bob hadn't dated many girls, and when they started talking about getting married, he knew deep down that he wasn't really ready. "But, like she said, we mostly played the game her way," he agrees. "I knew that she was the kind of girl I wanted to marry, and I wanted her to be the mother of my children, so I didn't want to risk losing her. Still, I was young, and there was so much I wanted to do and see."

A week before the ceremony, Bob's ambivalence gave him cold feet, and he told her so. Impetuously, Lorraine called the whole thing off . . . then two weeks later they ran off and got married anyway.

The timing was all wrong. "We really hurt my parents running off like we did," she says, shaking her head, "especially after all the plans had been made for a big wedding."

"Yeah," admits Bob, "and it certainly didn't make a very strong foundation on which to begin married life."

Lorraine believes they were meant for each other, but it wasn't long after they were married that she could see Bob was a restless soul. "Here was a man I realized I hardly knew even though we had dated for some time."

After three months of marriage, the "new" was gone. Bob was bored with the whole thing. Lorraine started being sick every morning, and he had a suspicion why. She was pregnant!

Bob leans back in his chair as he remembers those early days and smacks the heel of his hand to his forehead. "I sure wasn't ready for that! I said to myself, *I'm outta here!* — and I went down and joined the Marines for a four-year hitch."

Bob figured four years of frequently being apart would end up keeping them together. "I could see some country and maybe settle the restless feeling inside me. In the meantime, I could support Lorraine with my military pay, and she would be waiting for me at home."

But to Lorraine, Bob's joining the Marines was like running out on the marriage — and, as he later admitted, in a way it was. She developed a martyr attitude; after all, she had been raised to believe that marriage was something you stayed with no matter how bad it got.

Within a few months, Bob and Lorraine's marriage had brewed up a storm. It seemed like everything turned into a hassle. Bob remembers that it became a *habit* not to see eye-to-eye on almost everything. "We didn't know how to talk anything out. She would be hurt for days, and I would get silent. Then we'd make up by making love. We never solved anything. We just made beautiful babies."

Bob's silences frustrated Lorraine because she had been raised in a vocal family. But to Bob, arguments were simply not done.

His parents never did. So when they disagreed, he would leave the house; when he came back the subject was closed.

As Lorraine recalls, the next few years seem lost to her among all the moves required to keep up with the Marines, having gorgeous babies, raising healthy kids, being up day and night, concentrating on being a good mother, never going anywhere except to the store and church.

When Bob got out of the Marines after four years, he took second jobs — not just to help with the bills, but more, he admits, to get out of the house.

"My mother was a totally efficient woman," he says. "She more or less ran the family when I was growing up. Housekeeping and appearances meant everything to her. I expected Lorraine to be like her, but she didn't even come close. I wanted to come home to the kind of house my mother kept, but ours seemed like a constant mess. Dirty clothes were always piled in front of the washer and dryer, and it seemed like I could smell diapers everywhere."

Being a good mother meant something entirely different to Lorraine. "He wanted me to be Mrs. Clean. But to me, being a good mother meant rocking, reading, playing, and nurturing the children. Then I'd fit what had to be done around the house in between.

"Bob came from long generations of male chauvinists — on both sides," complains Lorraine. "Anything that needed doing in the house was 'woman's work.' I was shocked at how deeply ingrained that was. I couldn't even sneak in a few chores on him."

Lorraine suffered a kind of culture shock as she realized Bob's entire family had a different outlook on everything, even though their families' economic status was similar. "Men in my family helped with just about anything, so why did he think he was too good to do that?" says Lorraine. "Of course, secretly I knew that I was raised with the *right* point of view — he wasn't."

As a result, she remembers entering into what she calls "a real pity party that lasted for years." In time she began to feel that her talents and activities no longer mattered. She felt her entire personality was being shut up into a box, and she didn't know how to climb out. "I gained more weight with every baby — so that by number six I was a complete mess. In that way I took Bob for granted. Maybe I did it to get back at him for the put-downs about my housekeeping."

On the more positive side, both Lorraine and Bob considered their children the best part of their marriage. "I wasn't involved with them like I could have been," admits Bob, "but we didn't fight in front of them either. We tried to keep peace when they were in the room. She was good with the kids. I always respected her for the special love and patience she had with such a brood."

However, Bob stayed away from the house more and more, and the less Lorraine saw of him, the more starved she felt for adult conversation. "I sensed he wasn't proud of me anymore," she recalls. "He never took me anywhere — but then there really wasn't money to go anywhere, anyway. And he'd get so upset over bills that I'd end up feeling sorry for myself. I developed a habit of showing little or no emotion. He wasn't interested in the real me, so I never let it out. My sense of humor totally disappeared, and I used to have a pretty good one. An ugly sarcasm took its place. It was my defense mechanism."

The more time passed, the more Bob became obsessed with his dissatisfaction with Lorraine. Her problems were all he could see. "It seemed like she depended on me for her source of happiness," Bob rationalized. "I couldn't produce that. But she didn't seem like the girl I'd married, either — or the dream girl that I'd wanted."

Expectations abound with each of us — especially when it comes to our marriage partner. Clarifying expectations and negotiating roles is an ongoing marital challenge.

Marriage continues our maturity process, but not in the same way as our relationship with parents. Childhood maturing accepts a hierarchy or authoritarian structure. Parents guide, structure, supervise. Children respond, comply, obey . . . or, if they don't, consequences follow. Whether the parent-child relationship goes well or not, the parent was here first, is older, bigger, and legally in charge.

Marriages, however, are partnerships that start from scratch. Set structures are not readily agreed upon. The question of who is in charge is not as clear with couples as it is between parents and children. Therefore, each marriage must work out how the couples will share power and authority. Any married person who can recall the last time their spouse attempted to "make" them do something knows the uncomfortable feeling this creates.

Most marriages need outside support to remain healthy. Bob and Lorraine, however, did not have a mutually supportive network. They both grew up going to church, but when the hassle of getting kids ready to go on Sunday morning really started, Bob wanted no part of it. It estranged them further when Lorraine insisted on going. He viewed church as a waste of time. "After all," he'd complain, "what can you get out of it when all you're doing is trying to make the kids be still?"

What Lorraine found at church was not necessarily a support for her marriage, but a place where she could exercise her musical abilities and receive badly-needed compliments. "I was forever fishing for compliments from Bob but never catching any. It probably made me seem pitiful to him. But at church I didn't even have to hint around. People were always complimenting me on my talents."

The extended family, which can be a source of support for couples, did not benefit the Evans either. Bob's sisters were tiny, gorgeous blondes, and Lorraine felt that they doted on him. His mom would invite Bob over and take him out to give him a "bright spot" in his day. Bob's mother and sisters acted as though they felt sorry for his unhappy state and blamed Lorraine for it.

Their actions may have come out of a sense of love for him, Lorraine realizes, but it created an awful state of competition.

"There should have been no competition between us," she says, "but compete we did, and Bob was flattered by their loyalty while I was devastated by their implied condemnation."

But Bob's problems were certainly not all of Lorraine's making. He had gotten married young and ill-equipped to support the six children he fathered. They never seemed to have enough money. Bob felt inadequate to meet all the financial demands of a big family, let alone the need he felt to make Lorraine happy. He remembers feeling tied down, which he was, but it was largely his own doing. "Something in me was rising up and rebelling at that feeling," he recalls. "I wanted to be free! I could never see any success in having the things I wanted: a new home, a new car, a job I liked. They were always out of reach."

In the Bible, James the Apostle asked, "What causes fights and quarrels among you? Don't they come from your desires that battle within you? You want something but don't get it. You kill and covet, but you cannot have what you want. You quarrel and fight" (James 4:1-2). Bob did not go so far as to allow his restless desires to end in physical violence, but he did set in motion what he thought would be another means of escaping his situation.

At first Bob excused it as an unusual need for excitement. "I was born with it, I guess, but it's almost like a curse. Lorraine doesn't have it, and she didn't understand it. My desire for excitement drove me to hobbies I couldn't afford. I got into stock cars, dirt bikes, drag racing, and friends who liked the same things. I was 32 years old and saw my life as being nearly half over, and I wanted more out of it than I was getting. It was hard to explain."

And even harder for Lorraine to understand. "When he told me one day that his life was almost half over and there was so much more that he wanted to do — man! I couldn't see it. He'd been into drag racing, building stock cars, riding dirt bikes, hill climbing, hunting . . . on and on. I didn't understand that his cry came from a man who wanted a close, romantic relationship with a beautiful woman, but he didn't know how to drag that out of me, the mother of his children."

Finally Bob took more drastic measures to satisfy what he thought of as his "natural" restlessness. He got involved with another woman. "I wanted a new thrill, a new romance," he admits, shaking his head. "I didn't hate Lorraine; I just didn't feel anything. So when Michelle, a divorcee we both knew, started paying attention to me, I went for it. She represented — sort of — the fantasy I'd been hunting for. She was terribly good looking, had a new car, was self-employed. She said, 'No strings,' and that sounded good to me. She made it easy to escape from my problems. She knocked herself out for me, which flattered my ego. I never intended to break up my marriage or leave the family to marry her, but a relationship with her 'on the side' seemed okay. I had a right to some happiness, didn't I?"

Of course it wasn't okay with Lorraine! The day she realized that Bob had a lover, she pounced on that fact and named Michelle as the destroyer of their marriage. It was all her fault! Lorraine couldn't see that the breakdown had been in the making for a long, long time.

Cause and effect. We all thirst for an explanation to life's disappointments and things that go wrong. Unfortunately, our tendency is accurately described by Jesus' teaching: "Why do you look at the speck of sawdust in your brother's eye and pay no attention to the plank in your own eye?" (Matt. 7:3;NIV).

We all sin. That's not the point. It's where

we start that gets us nowhere. "You started it!" too often justifies a cycle in which inhumanity brings about more inhumanity. Push turns to shove.

As long as couples only see the faults of the other, progress stagnates. When a person feels that hurts warrant retaliation, the warfare continues. Two drowning swimmers, each pushing the other under, spells disaster for both.

The ironic thing was that just before the "end" came for Bob (justifying the affair in his mind), Lorraine thought things were better than they'd ever been! There would be no more babies, so *that* worry was over. They'd recently bought a newer house and the children were getting out of the baby stage. They were both crazy about the kids, and Lorraine hoped this would hold them together.

"I tried to wait the affair out," Lorraine recalls. "But in the process I turned into an insane-acting, jealous witch. I argued, trying to get him to change his mind. I was like a rubber ball on a string, crying one minute, plotting angry retaliations the next. I had feelings of not wanting to live."

Lorraine fought the inevitable, heartbreaking end of her marriage with every counter tactic she could dream up. "The pity of it," she realizes now, "was that as a couple we had waited until it was too late to begin trying to save it."

She finally realized Bob's feelings for her were basically dead. "And it showed," she says. "He was passive, even gentle, saying he didn't want to hurt me — but after we fought over the affair until it was hopeless, he said he really wanted out of the marriage, and nothing I did or said moved him."

Lorraine was frightened. She couldn't imagine being alone with six children. How would she support herself? To her, going on welfare seemed like an abomination.

To pursue his relationship with the other woman, Bob was often gone, and when he did come home, Lorraine cried and ranted and raved. A couple can't keep that behavior from the kids for very long. The Evans tried, but it became impossible.

Finally Lorraine drew a line in the sand: "It's either her or me!"

At the time, Michelle was conveniently there for him, and Bob enjoyed the new excitement she brought into his life. He wasn't ready to give her up. So when Lorraine told him to leave the house, he did.

"I hadn't started out intending to get divorced," says Bob. "But effective communication between Lorraine and me had become nonexistent — if it ever existed at all. I usually waited until I was really upset to confront her about whatever, and then my complaint would usually be met with a blank look and a shrug of the shoulders. To me that spelled out that she didn't care. Then, she was so mad over the affair, but I wasn't ready to repent, so trying to work anything out seemed hopeless."

Soon after moving out Bob filed for a divorce. It came through after about nine months. "Ironically," recalls Bob, "when it was final, I didn't feel like celebrating. I felt like a total failure. I wanted to crawl into a hole somewhere and stay.

"Though I'd grown up in a church-going family, I had stopped going to church, and at that point in my life, God seemed far, far away. Asking for His help seemed pointless. Lorraine had started going back to church, but all I could see was a bunch of hypocrites pointing a finger at what a dirty son-of-a-gun I was."

Bob had no intention of getting married again, but in what he calls a "weaker moment," he did. "On the spur of the moment," he says, "I married this woman I'd been living with.

"We soon achieved the look of success

— the house in the right neighborhood, the new car, the new pickup, and lots of going out on the town."

But there were also some big problems, problems not unrelated to what had made her so "available" in the first place. "Michelle needed her daily 'happy hour,' " recalls Bob. "That is, we got along better and our communication was better once she'd had a few drinks every evening. Otherwise it wasn't so hot."

Too late Bob realized that was no way to build a solid relationship, and before long the new marriage began to deteriorate. In despair, Bob concluded that he simply wasn't cut out to be a successful marriage partner for anybody. His first marriage had not brought happiness. And now his second attempt was in a tailspin. Even all the possessions that he'd accumulated while married to his new wife didn't seem to fulfill his longings like he'd expected. It was all a dead-end street.

Sooner or later we all have to face the person in the mirror. Someone to blame or distract us can keep us from self-reflection and maintain our self-destructive patterns. Every story of recovery in a marriage, however, begins in private . . . a lonely place where only God is present. When responsibility for the "plank in our own eye" is taken, and a desire for change is born.

Until the divorce, her marriage had seemed safe and secure to Lorraine. No matter how severe their fights, she believed that Bob would always be there for her. She liked being married and had refused to see that Bob had grown to not like it. She blamed everybody and everything for the failure of the marriage,

Even with six kids in the house, she never felt more lost and alone. The future seemed hopeless. They had no mutual friends, nothing working for them in a constructive way. Lorraine was also faced with how she was going to make ends meet financially. What was she going to do?

She began by trying every way imaginable to talk to Bob into changing his mind. She was frightened at the prospect of being the decision-maker, so she called him constantly for help with everything: the car, the TV, the bills. But instead of engaging him, it repulsed him.

Her pride was hurt. The sense of failure brought on depression, and for a time she functioned only for the kids' needs. "I ached physically for how deeply and truly I loved this man," she recalls. "In my heart, I felt I was a one-man woman, and right or wrong, good or bad, he was the only man I would ever love in this way."

But being left for someone else was the worse part to Lorraine. She felt it would have been easier to grieve the death of a loved one than to face the fact that her husband had left her for another woman.

"My sexual attractiveness — my power as a woman — was destroyed," she says. "I was angry at times. *How dare he do this to me?* I would dream up angry retaliations . . . then go through periods of not wanting to live. Then my feelings would do a flip-flop and I would ache physically for how much I loved him. Why couldn't I have shown him? Why couldn't he see?" It was as if her womanliness had never existed, and a sense of hopelessness threatened to overwhelm her.

For Lorraine, facing her contribution to the problems in her marriage began with the long-range task of rebuilding a damaged self-image. She went through a period of fixing herself up and going out. "I wanted to see if Bob's rejection of me was every man's opinion," she admits. "It wasn't long before I proved to myself that I still had what it took to make a man pay attention to me. But I quickly determined that this wasn't the way for me. I wasn't the bar-hopping type. I needed time to be objective about my intense love for my husband. A wise social worker told me it could take a couple of years."

Lorraine knew she needed some distance, and she realized that the only way she was going to quit trying to keep in touch with Bob was to move. So she sold their home and moved to be closer to the help and loving support of her own family. It was a good thing to do. "I had to do something about me," she says. "I wanted to feel okay. I wanted to find some positive strokes, and I wanted to be a woman Bob *could* love — whether he ever did again or not."

Two years passed after Lorraine moved without any contact between her and Bob. She was living in Kansas near her parents, and he was working in Colorado. Then on October 15, 1972, on Ray's twelfth birthday, he called his father. "He said he wanted to see me — no special reason — he just wanted to talk with his dad," remembers Bob. "Boy, that touched me. I knew a boy needs his father, and I wasn't there."

Bob felt pushed up against the wall. Lorraine had made it clear that he could only see the kids alone, meaning without Michelle with whom he was still living. But Michelle had predicted, "If you go alone, you won't come back." Knowing how precarious their relationship had become, Bob knew that might be true.

"I began to be weighted down with guilt for getting myself into such a foolish situation. My life was in pieces, pieces that I couldn't fit together. I wanted to be with my own kids, but I wasn't going to take the initiative to destroy what was left of my second marriage."

But in a few months, it ended anyway, and Bob moved into his own apartment. One of the first things he did was to call Lorraine. He hadn't talked to her in over two years. To his surprise, she was friendly on the phone. She let him talk to all of the kids, and said he could visit them anytime he wanted. But he was 500 miles away, and he told her he probably couldn't make it for a couple of months.

"The night that Bob called to say he was on his own again, I could hardly believe it," recalls Lorraine. "Ray had answered the phone and handed it to me saying that it sounded like Dad. 'You're crazy, too,' I said. But then this deep, gravelly voice on the other end of the line drawled, 'What's going on?'

"I almost squealed like a teenage girl.

He sounded so good, and he was so sweet and so considerate and such a gentleman. He wanted to come visit the kids — could he? Well, do cows eat grass? Of course he could come!"

Lorraine felt like she was being handed another chance, but being the intelligent person that she is, she didn't tell anyone what was on her mind. She also was smart enough to not say, "I told you so," when he told her that he was living alone. She just thanked God for answering a prayer that He had been listening to for a long time.

She made up her mind right then that if she ever got the chance, Bob was going to be loved, truly loved like he'd never been loved in all the years they had been married. He said he couldn't make it for a couple months, but Lorraine vowed she would make good use of the time.

During the two years since she'd last seen Bob, Lorraine's outlook on life had changed a lot. She had a job. She enjoyed being with the kids. She had developed a network of good friends, and she was making friends with herself. Even her humor was back. Life was a struggle at times, and it took a lot to make ends meet. She was not setting the world on fire by any means, but she had a nice apartment, a dependable car, and she was getting by.

"My real pride was in what neat people our kids were turning out to be," she says. "I still loved Bob, but I had tucked him away in a corner of my heart and was almost to the place where I could say being single wasn't the end of the world."

In terms of the kids, while Bob and Lorraine were apart she sent the kids' school pictures to him, she let them write to him, and occasionally she had let them call. She had made up her mind that she would never run him down to any of the kids, and she didn't let anyone else do it either. "They had a whole lifetime to figure out if he'd been a dirty rat or not on their own — with no help from me," she explains.

For his part, Bob had basically stayed out of the kids' lives out of love. And it often hurt him. He knew that every time he had come and gone from the house it had upset them greatly, and he didn't want to continue hurting them. Surprisingly, he also trusted Lorraine not to destroy his relationship with the kids. To the credit of both, neither Bob nor Lorraine destroyed or lost basic respect for each other in relation to their kids.

Stopping old patterns is essential. Starting to act out of a desire to be the person God created you to be takes courage. Dropping the emotional demands on the other person ends the power struggle. Can you "make" somebody love you? No. But you can become as healthy a person as possible. Bob and Lorraine had smashed the fantasies. They had punished each other as well as self-destructed. Now, the tug-of-war was over. No more "good guy" versus "bad guy." Just two humble people trying to stay afloat.

It did not take Bob two months to arrange a trip to Kansas. He found a way in less than three weeks.

Lorraine remembers: "One night we all came home late from the theater, and what should we find parked in front of our door but a big 750 motorcycle. Our youngest son who hadn't seen it for years yelled, 'Mom, that's my daddy's motorcycle!'

"Well, those wild kids baled out and were all over him. It was quite a sight, and I stood back and had a quiet conversation with God. It consisted of lots of thank Yous. I stayed in the background as much as possible. I didn't care how long it took, I knew that night there would be more visits, and they would be nice ones."

The biggest shock to Lorraine that weekend was when she saw Bob get his own coffee, empty his own ashtrays, and carry his own dishes to the sink. Suddenly she began to believe that Bob could change after all. Maybe it shouldn't be so surprising, she told herself; she had changed, too. It was a promising beginning.

There was lots of time to get acquainted all over again . . . for everybody. Bob knew there would be many difficult memories to work through and put at rest, but first he and Lorraine had to become friends. Once they had been lovers, but never friends. Now he sensed they were both ready for friendship.

For the next year, Bob got acquainted with every inch of the highway between Colorado and Kansas as he rode his bike to see his family every few weekends. The kids treated him as though he'd never been gone. He recalls that they were good, well-behaved kids and hadn't been turned against him. He was grateful for that. During that period, the kids made his world go round.

Eventually Bob's work all but ended in Colorado, so near the end of that year he moved to relocate closer to the kids. He soon was spending every weekend with them. At that point he was just "spending time with the kids," but he also began to notice how easy it was to be there. The kids were forever asking if Lorraine could go with them wherever they went, and Bob began saying, "Sure," without having a catch in his stomach wondering if things would break down.

Now he smiles as he remembers, "She was easy to be with, easy to talk to, and a lot of fun. We were becoming very good friends. I began to notice that we rarely had hassles about anything. Maybe we were mellowing. I even went to church with them because the kids wanted me to. I didn't particularly care about what people thought about this strange set-up. The weird thing was that Lorraine didn't seem to care what people thought either. Earlier I had thought she lived her whole life trying to make things look good to the church people."

During his visits, Lorraine noticed that Bob was more and more tolerant of including her. Naturally she wanted to be with him and the kids, but she didn't want to overwhelm him with any assumptions. So when it was his time to be with the kids, she always waited for his invitation. Soon it became, "Well, what are you waiting for? Come on!"

One of the things Lorraine was working on was learning to behave honestly. Earlier she had often made jokes about things that were hurtful to her. It had been a way of coping in her childhood family, and she was a champion at it.

But as they were becoming re-acquainted, she began to remember all the times Bob had accused her of not caring, and she began to see — in her quiet times of reflection — that her way of avoiding pain had been to make a joke of it. Now she was going to have to take a risk in being real.

"When I was happy, it was easy to act real," she says. "I showed it when I was grateful. I tried to show it when I was genuinely concerned. But when I was hurt — that was the toughest. I had always played silly little games. But as I began being honest, I was amazed how well Bob responded. He began to be honest right back. He began to share with me some real stuff, stuff I'd never heard about what really made him tick."

One example had to do with how it made him feel when she expected him to be someone he wasn't. It was one thing for him to learn to share in doing the household chores, but it was something else to expect him not to enjoy thrilling sports like mountain biking. The first involved becoming more considerate of others; the second expected him to deny his nature. "I threw all my old expectations out the window," says Lorraine, "all the images of what I wanted him to be like. He would never be like anybody I knew. Besides, I decided I liked his individuality. I let him know that what he was and how he was and who he was, just like he was — was all right with me."

For Lorraine, the most challenging adjustment involved coming to terms with "the other woman." They had to sort through what was Lorraine's responsibility and what was Bob's. "Forgiveness is a decision, not a feeling," observes Lorraine. "There are circumstances that I will never forget, but giving those hurting memories to the Lord and making a decision to leave the hurt with Him eases the pain with that memory. When the temptation comes to retaliate and hurt back by bringing up old, forgiven wrongs, I concentrate on complementing, loving, and thanking God for what is now."

After about a year of getting reacquainted, becoming better friends, and dealing with some of the old hurts, Bob suggested that they get remarried. "I wanted to be with the kids full time, and Lorraine and I had become very comfortable together. At the time, I could see her depth of feeling for me was much deeper than I felt for her, and

I didn't lie to her about that. But I believed that my love could grow — I made up my mind that it would. We eight pieces of a puzzle fit together, and it felt good to be a family."

For Bob, putting the marriage back together was mostly making decisions and not letting the upsetting times rule him. With a crooked smile he says, "I'm not the easiest guy in the world to live with. I realize that, but I've learned to calm down, especially when I'm angry. When the discussion gets heated, I try to back off and give Lorraine time to answer. She can't respond — or won't — to loud demands."

Both Bob and Lorraine have learned to give each other some space to be the individuals that they are. Bob sees Lorraine as a people-person, the proverbial "do-gooder," and that sometimes drives him nuts. "But I'm trying to let her do her own thing because it makes her happier," he says. "And when I see her trying to curtail some of it out of respect for me, I let her know I appreciate it."

Though both Bob and Lorraine had imagined that they were good lovers (if not very good friends) when they were first married, they made the effort to educate themselves so that they could be the best lovers they could possible be the second time around. They found that good sex didn't necessarily happen spontaneously. They discovered some excellent books written on the subject. Smart is always better than dumb, and no one is a mind reader, so they learned to talk and ask each other what they wanted in a lover. "We found that the miracle of love can make a vast difference in one's fantasies, and in our case it did," says Lorraine.

In the next year after remarrying, Bob and Lorraine made new friends that accepted them together as a couple. They began attending church together, and that had a remarkably solidifying effect. They attended a marriage seminar together that taught good basic principles for marriage — something they had never been exposed to in all their years of married life before.

Their parents — his and hers — finally became a tremendous support system for them. They wanted to see the family survive. When the extended families saw that Lorraine and Bob were serious about making a go of it, they became a positive force. "Bob's mom still dotes on him," says Lorraine, "but it doesn't divide us anymore. We can laugh about it because she's not doing it because she feels sorry for him."

One of the things they worked hard on

was regaining their sense of humor. "We had quit laughing," remembers Bob. "Everything was so dead serious before we separated. I could go out with my friends and have a great weekend, but we couldn't seem to do that together. One of the things that I did wrong was not trying to work out how to have fun together. After we got married again, we made that a priority."

Downward spirals are hard to stop. But an upward, positive momentum is powerful, too. Openness responded to with understanding builds intimacy. Caring for each other builds trust. Supportive actions build gratitude. The flow of love — real, honest, committed — leads to a bond of hope.

The bonds of a loving, growing relationship take work, but the rewards re-energize. Destructive, dysfunctional patterns drain us. Positive interactions rebuild, repair, and renew.

This was life for the newly remarried Evans on the morning of August 8, 1976. It was a good life filled with hope; the pieces of their puzzle were coming together. By that afternoon, it was blown apart by the train accident that killed four of their children: two boys and two girls.

Bob raced home from Oklahoma after hearing the tragic news. Life was an unreal swirl of making funeral arrangements, visiting Troy in the hospital, and waiting anxiously for the doctors to report. Neither Bob nor Lorraine can remember much about that first week.

Again Bob told Lorraine, "Don't try and hang onto me for your support because I'm doing all I can to get one foot in front of the other. I can't drag you along. I feel lucky when I can force myself to get up in the morning."

"But who can I turn to?" Lorraine asked desperately.

"I don't know — your folks, friends, church people — anybody but me because I'm not that strong. I can't provide you with a life raft."

Though both Bob and Lorraine felt like the crisis was tearing them apart, they were too overwhelmed to care. But as the days of agony turned into weeks, and weeks into months, Bob was more supportive than he might have been during their first marriage.

Lorraine explains: "Bob had been raised in a 'men-don't-cry' tradition, but he had changed, and he really demonstrated that with our two remaining sons. There were times when he was hurting so much, but he didn't shut them out. He would have one on each knee with tears running down his face. I felt that was healthy, and they needed to see that."

That was a big change for Bob. He says, "I was raised in the model of my father and grandfather who were also strong, silent types. Men did not show their emotions. They locked their jaws and got through what they had to get through and ignored their emotions. That was what I grew up with, so it was hard to change that in me."

But the difference was far more supportive to Lorraine than if Bob had been able to forge ahead in his old, "strong," stoic style. "Even though Bob said he couldn't carry me through," recalls Lorraine, "he never left me. In fact, we would sit and just cry together, and in that way he was more support to me than if he had been the macho man who could gut it out and be my strong pillar giving me all the answers. If he had tried to give me answers, I would have felt abandoned rather than helped, because, in a way, there were no answers.

"Also," adds Lorraine, "we figured out right away with the boys that if we didn't keep talking, we were all going to sink."

Then one day one the boys said, "Are we always going to be sad?" Lorraine felt almost like he had hit her, and she realized that they couldn't raise those boys like that. The boys still had to get up in the morning and go to school. They had to have some normalcy in their lives. So she began to remember and speak of the fun things about the kids who had died.

"Even though it would make us cry," adds Bob, "we could also laugh about them. For a while we went through a period when we hesitated to even mention their names, but we couldn't live that way. They were still a part of us, they were just living in heaven."

So by crying together, talking together, and finally learning to laugh together again, the Evans made it through the next few years.

But there was another emotion they had to deal with — anger.

Lorraine says, "I was so mad at God that I thought my insides were coming out. How dare He take my children! But I learned a valuable lesson: God can take yelling at. It's even a form of prayer. I had a lot of insomnia. I would walk around downstairs in the middle of the night and yell a lot of 'Why?' questions at God and bang on the table and give God these long, long lists of why I didn't deserve this. After all, I had been teaching Sunday school that very morning my children had been killed. 'Don't I deserve better treatment than this?' I would say. I was supposed to be a loved child of God, and, hey, this was not fair.

"Finally, I made some new friends, three women who had lost loved ones, and I was able to talk to them. But they weren't in my church. I was getting an awful lot of pat answers from people in our church: 'Just turn it all over to the Lord,' or 'Just pray about it, and it'll all be better,' or 'You really shouldn't be angry like this.' It seemed that no one understood the anger part.

"Many days I felt like I was going crazy, and I would even say that I was. There were times when I felt like two people: On one hand I knew that my children were in heaven and I would see them again some day. On the other hand I bore those children into the world, and I had also buried them in the cemetery — and those two realities were in great conflict with each other. That didn't come together for a very long time, and it didn't come as a result of some great revelation or kernel of truth that someone told me. Those realities just slowly grew until I could accept both."

Bob remembers that in a time of overwhelming grief, mundane responsibilities seemed like cruel intrusions. But in a way they were gifts that kept him going. "For me," he reflects, "finding the strength to get through the grief came partially by putting one foot ahead of the other, doing what had to be done. Somehow I knew that keeping my job was still important for keeping what was left of the family together.

"Boy, there were sometimes when driving that old truck down the road, the tears would be coming so fast that I could barely see, but I kept going. I never considered that I had an option not to. I prayed a lot on the road, crying 'Why, Lord, why?'

"Every morning when I headed off to Kansas City — I was still driving the franchise food service route — I prayed that the Lord would keep my family safe while I was gone. But at the same time I was praying, there was this haunting memory that on that one dreadful Sunday He *hadn't* kept them safe. So why pray? I was angry and not sure God could be trusted anymore.

"I didn't give up on God — who else could I turn to? But it took years to feel like I could trust Him again. It is one thing to say it with your mouth, but to actually feel it in your heart walks a pretty narrow line."

There was one other thing that Bob did

to deal with his anger. Lorraine can laugh about it now, but at the time she says she was nearly ready to divorce him over it.

"Once Troy was out of the hospital and had his strength back, Bob got both boys dirt bikes. Of course, he had one, too. They rode those things like they were wild men across the rolling pastures and through the streams. They would drive themselves for hours until they would come in exhausted and covered with mud. It was a real physical thing that allowed him to put his intense feelings somewhere instead of taking them out on me or the family. I guess they took their feelings out on the bikes. But it scared me. I thought he was going to kill my last two kids."

"Now, Lorraine," Bob remonstrates with a smile, "it wasn't that bad. We were in a soft alfalfa field, after all, and that's a lot different than going down on asphalt or slamming into an oncoming car. Even before we got those bikes for the boys, I loved trail riding. I did a lot of hill climbing. It's very physical, and there's fairly rough terrain around our place. I would go out and just ride that bike as hard as it would go, jumping over logs and doing seemingly impossible things. I would go flat out like there was no tomorrow. I suppose that was one way of dealing with my anger and frustration and hurt. And it was a way to be close to the boys, too."

Destructive forces come in a wide variety. Sometimes they are slow and subtle. Other times they are sudden and overwhelming. Either way, rebuilding takes time. Quick fixes involving denial, escapism, and blame stand ready to lead us down a path of self-destruction.

Experiencing the total, body-crushing impact of emotional sorrow is slow going. Hope for a pain-free day is hard to come by. Maintaining a healing process in which the full emotional impact of the event is experienced and expressed is not our natural choice. By God's grace, however, Lorraine and Bob stayed on track. Beaten up by life's most crushing blows led to rivers of tears and heartache. But God sustained them.

In time comfort comes if we work through each experience. There are no easy answers. No short cuts. In the end we are stripped away of everything but the faith that through it all God's love will prevail.

About the time that Bob and Lorraine began to think that they were going to make it, they faced another challenge.

Troy had been born with a defective valve in his heart that the doctors said would eventually have to be replaced. They recommended keeping an eye on him, but waiting until he was 17 or 18 years old before replacing it with a metal valve. That way they could avoid a series of operations to put in larger and larger valves to keep up with his growth.

Troy had spent nearly a month in the hospital recovering from his injuries following the train accident. A couple months later, when he was nine and a half, Bob and Lorraine took him back to the hospital for his regular checkup on his heart valve. At that time his recovery from the accident seemed nearly complete.

However, the doctors found an aneurysm (a balloon-like swelling) in his ascending aorta, the main artery coming out of the top of the heart. They recommended an operation in the near future to repair it. (Some years later, the Evans learned that in high-impact crashes, the heart — a heavy organ that is not directly attached to the skeleton — can jerk the arteries by which it somewhat hangs and create just such an aneurysm. Therefore, it is likely that Troy's new problem resulted from the accident.)

The doctors explained that if the aneurysm burst, there would be no saving Troy. He would bleed to death in a minute or so.

Just before Christmas, the doctors operated and, among other things, put a graft in Troy's descending aorta taking some of the pressure off the aneurysm in the ascending aorta. Six months later he underwent another open-heart surgery to make further repairs which the doctors felt at that time took care of the danger.

Still, Troy's defective valve had not been replaced.

Six years later, when he was junior in high school, he began having some unusual pain in his back along with other symptoms that caused the Evans to take him in to check his heart. The aneurysm had redeveloped, so the doctors operated, replaced his heart valve, and put a graft on his ascending aorta, and sewed him back up. They felt that all the problems were cared for. It was the final solution, and Troy seemed to recover swiftly.

Ten days after the surgery Troy came home. It was a Wednesday. Somehow the blood thinners that Troy was on got out of balance, and his blood became so thin that it leaked through the new valve to the point where it blew off the new graft.

He died on Saturday.

"In some ways," says Lorraine, "my rage

over Troy's death was deeper than after the train accident. I guess I thought I had received more than my share of pain. Why more?

"One thoughtless friend said, 'Well, at least you've gone through this before,' meaning it shouldn't be so hard this time. But I can tell you, it was much worse. I knew how many years it had taken to go through the grief after the death of our other four children, and I dreaded the process."

This time it became too much for Lorraine. She tried to go back to work, but by June she "hit the wall." She couldn't go to work, she broke out in hives, and she could barely keep up with her duties around the house.

Her psychiatrist explained that stress can be cumulative, and there is a limit to how much a person can take. Lorraine had exceeded her limit. Fortunately, Bob was able to keep going until Lorraine recovered enough to go back to work.

But then something similar happened to him. "I was fortunate to have a very understanding boss," explains Bob. "I think he was a gift from God. I had ridden my motorcycle in to work one morning and had gone through a small rain shower. They don't usually bother me, but when I got into the office I was shaking like a leaf and couldn't calm down. I said to my boss, 'I don't know what's going on here, but I don't think I'm in any condition to be on the highway in my truck.' After talking to me a little, he sent me to a motel and said when I felt better to go home. He'd hold my job.

"I was out of work for eight weeks before I could go back. I don't know why he was so gracious at the time, but years later one of his daughters was killed, and at her funeral he said, 'Now I understand.' "

"We learned some valuable lessons through all these tragedies," says Lorraine. "If we had acted on our feelings, we wouldn't have had a prayer of survival because our emotions were totally out of control. But we didn't run away. Bob has been there for me when I had nothing to give back, and I think he would say the same about me. We tried not to direct all that hideous hurt at each other.

"Somehow we knew that the deadness of our feelings wouldn't last forever. Maybe it was instinct that told us that. I remember saying, 'God, can't You make it five years from now?' I somehow knew that down the road I would again feel something other than the intense pain that tragedy brought us.

"And that has happened," Lorraine smiles. "Today this marriage has such precious value to me. I know I've worked hard for it to be good. I hold Bob as a treasure in my hands. I want to know him better everyday. I've decided to make it my life's work to just do exactly that."

Bob takes Lorraine's hand and says quietly, "You know, the truth is, we are damaged. We will never be the same again. But our marriage is strong. I've grown to deeply love and respect this woman. We've walked hand in hand, shoulder to shoulder, right through the middle of hell. She's stuck with me like glue. Sometimes she knows me so well, it's like she's crawled inside my head and has taken a look around. She's my best friend. She makes loving her easy to do.

"Now we have only one child, Tyler. In a way, he helped us when we saw that we needed to help him. Troy's death shattered him, and we had to rally around to help him get back on his feet . . . whether we felt like it or not. He got involved in wrestling and went to the state championships and later got a wrestling scholarship to college. We supported him all the way and went to all his meets.

"Now, at 26, he's an electrical and mechanical engineer working for a tool-making company. He loves the Lord and is the delight of our lives.

"In the Bible," says Bob as he leans back in his chair, "there was a man by the name of Job who, after he lost his whole family, said of God, 'Though he slay me, yet will I trust in him' (Job 13:15). I can't tell you how to get to that kind of trust if you've been through something like we have. Even now — years later — I sometimes lose my focus. But if you give it time and keep turning *to* God rather than away from Him, it slowly comes."

Chapter Three

God Can Overcome the Odds

By Stephen Wilke, Ph.D.

"The odds of success" is a phrase that comes from short-term, worldly thinking. A world that weighs visible resources. A world focused on predicting marital bliss on one's money in the bank, house, car, job, and the beauty of the wedding. A world focused on the selection of the "right" man or woman, with the "right" compatibility of interests, activities, and family backgrounds. A world focused on feeling good and being a winner by doing things right.

The couples sharing in this book started off wrong; the odds were against them. Their marriages were ill-timed. Preparation was poor and maturity was low, with little foundation for a secure future. Not only that, but traumatic childhoods place enormous burdens on marriage. Devastating traumas can blow couples apart. Years of pain, loneliness, and despair can easily erode all love for self and spouse. Layers of guilt, anger, and frustration can dominate the emotional landscape.

In these kinds of situations the world says "cut your losses," "be free," "run from the pain." But these couples didn't listen to the world; they responded to a deeper voice. I believe they responded to God . . . against all the odds.

Let's examine some of what God said as revealed in these couples' lives:

Stronger Than the Odds

The human odds are not in our favor. The human race is riddled with enough tragedy, violence, and destructive sinfulness to have extinguished itself several times by now. On the personal level, every marriage certainly has enough unmet expectations to provide either spouse a case for dissatisfaction. Nobody is the perfect spouse and nobody marries the perfect Mr. or Mrs. Right. Marriage is often two wounded soldiers helping each other through a battlefield. Our emotional needs are often unclear to us and our spouse. Our perceptive abilities are primitive. Our

responsiveness is usually slow. Our human-
ness abounds in and around us. And yet. . . .

God says He is the supplier of forces
stronger than our own, stronger than the
world's. God redefines the odds. God provides a state of grace in which resources for
life are freely given. God breaks cycles of
abuse with healing. God sustains when one
is emotionally shattered. God cuts through
family secrets, pushing for truth. God provides a new day. The forces of God working
through the Holy Spirit stay with us, every
day . . . day after day . . . for all times . . .
ready and available!

God's Covenant — Forgiveness, Hope, and Love

The pain of life often pushes us into hiding. Self-protection becomes paramount.
Some people turn rough, hard, callused. Others become fragile and withdrawn. But self-
protection creates an emotional isolation. In
isolation we lose hope. Without hope, love
dies and there seems to be no way out.

The recovery process, for couple after
couple, begins with some break in the isolation. Moving out of isolation may begin
within. Perhaps new internal awareness of
old lies, hurts, and pain begins a healing pro-

cess. Others begin by opening up with other persons. Some start on the path with a spiritual reconnecting with God.

Regardless of the starting place, a complete recovery process involves forgiveness — given and received — and open, honest revelation of thoughts, feelings, and actions. Forgiveness is a decision growing out of a desire to experience cleansing. This desire causes us to expose and heal rather than to simply hide and self-protect. Forgiveness involves changes in one's view about himself or herself, in relationship with other persons, and with God.

Throughout our life experiences, God's covenant surrounds us. With even the smallest experience of forgiveness, persons can generate the hope to take the next step and move forward. With hope, a little vulnerability can be chosen. Choosing to be vulnerable in sharing thoughts and feelings makes it possible to *receive* support and love. Choosing to be vulnerable in listening to others makes it possible to *give* support and love. For forgiveness, hope, and love are relational; they cannot function in isolation. Only in the exchange of giving and receiving are forgiveness, hope, and love active. This activating exchange occurs between our current self-awareness and our past childhood self; ourselves and others; ourselves and God.

God's Path to Joy Is Truth

Hiding from the truth is our human way. Adam and Eve provide example NUMBER ONE. Millions upon millions of examples have followed. Feelings of shame, guilt, anger, inadequacy, and disobedience beg us to run for darkness and hide. And we do. Our list of hiding places is long and comprehensive. Each personality and background helps to customize the hiding place. Within marriage the hiding often takes on contrasting styles, creating a stand-off. One spouse hides behind self-righteous blame, the other behind disruptive behaviors. One hides behind an armor of outward strength, while the other hides behind helplessness and immaturity. One attacks, while the other retreats. One controls, while the other rebels. One externalizes, while the other internalizes.

The power of truth is actualized when a person comes out of hiding. Each person must tell his or her own story. So often in marriage we want to document the "truth" for our spouse. We want to provide the what, why, and wherefore of the other person's life. But healing truth doesn't work that way. Each person must do his or her own confession.

The biblical narrative is clear; personal testimony confirms it: "The truth shall set you free." But it is so very hard. The innocent accident, the honest mistake, the casual untruthfulness, and the willfully wrong act — all blackmail us into seclusion. God's hope is finding the courage to recognize the faraway land where we've been hiding and to return home like the Prodigal Son. For, in truth, the daily healing of our lives can replace fear with joy.

Strength to Face Our Fear

When we hear of people who face incredible odds, we often say, "I could never do that." "I don't know how they do it." "I would just die if that happened to me." We examine our resources and come up short. We are overwhelmed. Emotional pain panics us. In our despair, we assume nothing and nobody can help. *Our* spouse will never change. *Our* problems will never go away.

Fear is a paralyzing emotion. Fear stops marital, spiritual, and emotional growth. Fear says, "Let's die now and get it over with." But persons wishing to build a better marriage must look fear straight in the eye. Overcoming fear may have dramatic moments when major, highly-charged secrets are exposed. However, fear is also overcome in a daily attitude of openness and honest communication. Truthful self-examination and responsiveness to feedback help us to remember that God provides strength greater than fear. God's abundant future is possible. While we only get a daily supply of rations, they are sufficient for our journey.

Faithfulness Is Rewarded with Faith

Unfortunately, because we're only human, we want to say: "If I'm open and truthful, I want to know I'll get what I want." Anxiety around the cause and effect of our actions is a result of relational brokenness. When we're hiding, we don't know what will happen when we are found. Everyone wants to jump ahead and see the outcome without going through the process.

Real healing, however, requires faithful action. Faithfulness is the self-discipline of truthful living. While everything inside our head may be saying, "You're wasting your time . . . health and wholeness will never come . . . God has abandoned you . . . trying will get you nowhere," faithfulness dares us to take another step. *Steps of faithfulness are steps that go against the odds.* Accept that God can and will forgive you and your spouse and renew you both with hope and love. Build on truthful understanding and awareness. Depend on strength sufficient for the day.

With each faithful step, the reward is — more faith. More confidence in self, others, and God. The power of the two couples who share their journeys in this book is that they endured all of the emotional stages and phases of married life. Each had times when one tried while the other gave up. They had times when neither one could try and they were adrift. And they also experienced both taking steps of faith, hope, and love in step with each other.

Through it all, they remind us of enduring, spiritual truths: God's loving, healing Spirit is calling us to wholeness today. The resources we need are still in abundant supply. The repairing and renewing power of God continues to go against the odds and prevail.

Are these couples perfect? Oh, no! Are they still on a mysterious journey of fear and joy? Oh, yes! Walking as a couple in the ways of the Lord does not remove the challenges of this world.

But it does change the odds.

Chapter Five

What Is Recovery of Hope?

Recovery of Hope is a program for couples who are experiencing disillusionment in their marriages. Some may be contemplating divorce. The program recognizes that problems and disillusionment are normal in a marriage. However, many couples give up because they do not know what else to do.

Couples register for a three-hour session where a team of three alumni couples share their own experiences of disillusionment and the events and insights that created a spark of hope for them to attempt reconciliation. The new couples then consider their situation and how they are feeling about it. To aid in reaching a decision, a counselor will meet with the couple to help them tailor a plan to meet their needs. The reconciliation plan may include such things as counseling, meeting with a support group, programs for help in planning finances, parenting, and/or any other service which would be helpful.

ROH is based on sound psychological principles and basic spiritual values, along with acceptance and support from volunteers and professionals. It provides a couple with time to review their marriage and make a decision about their future. While ROH is forthright in being "pro-marriage," participants' decisions are honored and respected.

If you feel like giving up on your marriage, you may wish to contact the Recovery of Hope Network. To find the program nearest you, call (800) 327-2590 in the U.S. and Canada.